done in a day

Moab

→ The 10 Premier Hikes!

Where to invest your limited hiking time
to enjoy the greatest scenic reward

by KATHY + CRAIG COPELAND

hikingcamping.com

Heading outdoors eventually leads you within.

The first people on earth were hikers and campers. So today, when we walk the earth and bed down on it, we're living in the most primitive, elemental way known to our species. We're returning to a way of life intrinsic to the human experience. We're shedding the burden of millennia of civilization. We're seeking catharsis. We're inviting enlightenment.

hikingcamping.com publishes unique guidebooks – literate, entertaining, opinionated – that ensure you make the most of your precious time outdoors. Our titles cover some of the world's most spectacular wild lands.

To further support the community of hikers, campers, and cyclists, we created www.hikingcamping.com. Go there to connect with others who share your zeal, to plan your next trip, or to stay inspired between trips. Get advice from people returning from your destination, or share tips from your recent adventure. And please send anything you want to post that will assist or amuse the rest of us.

To fully benefit from, and contribute to, the book you're now reading, visit www.hikingcamping.com and follow this path: Guidebooks > Hiking > Utah Canyon Country > Done in a Day: Moab > Field Reports.

nomads@hikingcamping.com   **hiking camping**.com

MEMBER 1% FOR THE PLANET

Businesses donating
1% of their sales to the
natural environment

www.onepercentfortheplanet.org

printed on recycled paper

Copyright © 2008
by Craig and Kathy Copeland
First edition, February 2008

**Published in Canada by
hikingcamping.com, inc.
P.O. Box 8563
Canmore, Alberta, T1W 2V3 Canada**
nomads@hikingcamping.com

All photos by the authors

Maps and production by C.J. Chiarizia
giddyupgraphics@mac.com

Cover and interior design
by www.subplot.com

Printed in China by Asia Pacific Offset

Library and Archives Canada Cataloguing in Publication

Copeland, Kathy, 1959-
    Moab: the 10 premier hikes / by Kathy & Craig Copeland.
(Done in a day)

Includes index.   ISBN 978-0-9735099-8-4

        1. Hiking--Utah--Moab--Guidebooks. 2. Trails--Utah--Moab--
Guidebooks. 3. Moab (Utah)--Guidebooks. I. Copeland, Craig, 1955-
II. Title. III. Series: Copeland, Kathy, 1959- Done in a day.

GV199.42.U82M633   2007 796.5220979258   C2007-902714-8

Contents

TRIPS AT A GLANCE

Trips are listed according to difficulty, starting with the easiest and working up to the most challenging. After the trip name is the round-trip distance, followed by the elevation gain.

1	Corona Arch	3 mi (5 km)	556 ft (170 m)
2	Morning Glory Canyon	4.6 mi (7.4 km)	327 ft (100 m)
3	Fisher Towers	4.6 mi (7.4 km)	1050 ft (320 m)
4	Mary Jane Canyon	8.7 mi (14 km)	410 ft (125 m)
5	Big Spring & Squaw Canyons	7.5 mi (12.1 km)	430 ft (131 m)
6	Devils Garden	7.7 mi (12.4 km)	650 ft (198 m)
7	Murphy Hogback	9.75 mi (15.7 km)	1240 ft (378 m)
8	Peekaboo	10 mi (16.2 km)	940 ft (287 m)
9	Upheaval Canyon	8 mi (12.9 km)	1480 ft (451 m)
10a	The Needles	5.6 mi (9 km)	770 ft (235 m)
10b	Chesler Park / Joint	11.1 mi (17.9 km)	910 ft (277 m)
10c	Devils Kitchen	10.5 mi (16.9 km)	1060 ft (323 m)
10d	Druid Arch	10.8 mi (17.4 km)	880 ft (268 m)
10a-b-d combined		15.3 mi (24.6 km)	1430 ft (436 m)

Porcupine Rim

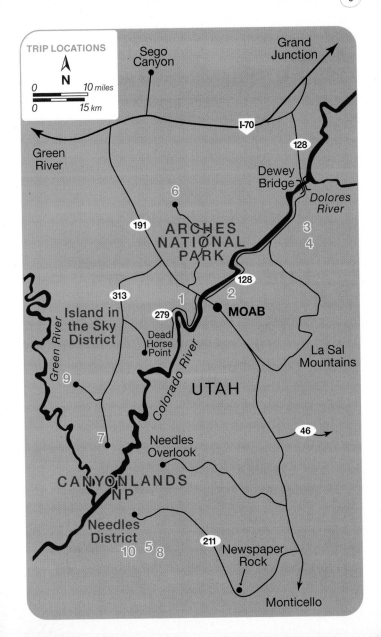

TRIP LOCATIONS

N

0   10 miles
0   15 km

Sego Canyon

Grand Junction

I-70

Green River

128

Dewey Bridge

Dolores River

6

191

ARCHES NATIONAL PARK

3
4

128

313

1

2

MOAB

279

Island in the Sky District

Dead Horse Point

Green River

La Sal Mountains

UTAH

9

Colorado River

7

46

Needles Overlook

CANYONLANDS NP

Needles District

10 5 8

211

Newspaper Rock

Monticello

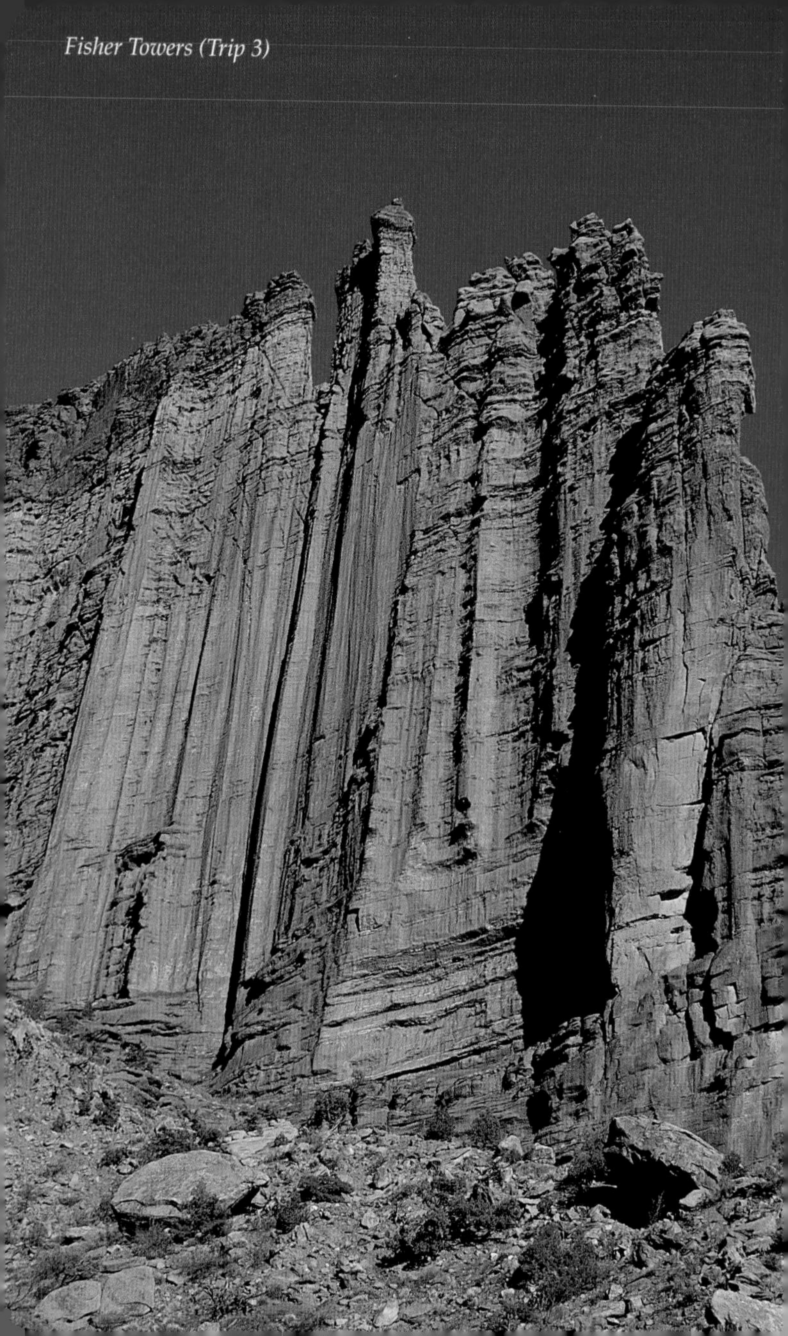

Fisher Towers (Trip 3)

WOW

Your time is short, but the canyons are endless. So here you go: the ten Moab-area dayhikes most likely to make you say "Wow!" Plus our boot-tested opinions: why we recommend each trail, what to expect, how to enjoy the optimal experience.

We hope our suggestions compel you to get outdoors more often and stay out longer. Do it to cultivate your wild self. It will give you perspective. Do it because the backcountry teaches simplicity and self-reliance, qualities that make life more fulfilling. Do it to remind yourself why wilderness needs and deserves your protection. A bolder conservation ethic develops naturally in canyon country. And do it to escape the cacophony that muffles the quiet, pure voice within.

Where Exactly?

To find the town of Moab on a map, trace the Utah-Colorado border from bottom to top. Stop just below the midpoint and follow the Colorado River slightly left (southwest).

By car, it's 460 mi (742 km) north of Phoenix (an 8-hour drive), 234 mi (377 km) southeast of Salt Lake City (a 4-hour drive), or 355 mi (571 km) west of Denver (a 5½-hour drive).

The nearest substantial airport is a 113-mi (182-km), 2-hour drive east, in Colorado, at Grand Junction's Walker Field (GJT). Flight times are 3½ hours from Los Angeles (LAX), 4 hours from Seattle (SEA), 4½ hours from Calgary (YYC), and less than 4 hours from Dallas (DFW).

Welcome to Moab, Utah: latitude 38° 34' 21" N, longitude 109° 32' 59" W, elevation 4,025 feet (1227 meters).

Hike First, Read Later

Because our emphasis here is efficient use of limited time, we don't expect you to read the rest of this introduction.

Not immediately, anyway.

Beyond page 56 it's not necessary, unless you're a novice canyon-country hiker or tentative in new territory.

We resent guidebooks that begin with a perfunctory *How To Use This Book* section. As if it were required reading. As if books were a strange, new marvel. We assume you feel the same.

If you're seasoned and confident, we figure you'll flip to the ten premier hikes, then dash onto the trail of your choice, just as we would.

Read or hike? No contest. The greatest book of all is the earth itself. Going on a hike is a way of turning the pages.

But before Moab is in your rearview mirror, keep reading. At least through page 56.

It won't take long. And what you learn will top-up your understanding of a place that's going to be on your mind a long, long time after you leave.

A Vast Earthen Sculpture

Humans can't survive without dreaming. Deprived of our nightly flights of imagination, our sanity disintegrates. Likewise, deprived of mystery, our soul withers.

Some think they need only answers. But the need for mystery is greater than the need for any answer.

And just as sleeping summons our dreams, hiking is an invocation to mystery. Especially if we're hiking in the most mysterious land of all: the vast, earthen sculpture known as *southeast Utah*.

The soaring arches, bulging walls, towering spires, and fiery colors eventually, inexorably lull hikers into a state of contemplation in which we ponder and are strangely soothed by life's enduring mysteries.

Western edge of the Slickrock Trail, overlooking the Colorado River and Arches National Park

We're aware of the scientific view. We've heard about the processes that shaped this topography. What geologists tell us makes sense. We don't question *how*. We wonder *why*. We seek a transcendent explanation.

Could aimless physics really be responsible for creating such a bizarre and sensuous wonderland? Or was there intent? The intent to inspire play and elicit joy among all creatures who wander here?

Romping like children—across slickrock, into labyrinthian canyons—we sense nature's intent. It ignites our curiosity, powers our limbs. But such a profound experience is ineffable. The standard tourism vocabulary fails.

Vacation? Hiking into a raw, bone-naked desert that subverts our very concept of this blue-green planet is no mere vacation. It's a catharsis.

Scenery? It's a pale word for the natural phantasmagoria that grace this land.

Friendly people? Mingling with the souls of Ancestral Puebloan Indians in a silent, red-rock alcove is a journey to another realm and cannot be measured in such mundane terms.

Many authors have explored the mysterious appeal of canyon country. Edward Abbey remains the most famous, though Terry Tempest Williams is more deeply illuminating.

The residents of Moab—ranchers, bike mechanics, shop owners, miners, tour guides, hoteliers, artists—have also riffed on the mystery of their homeland. They did it en masse when a local bookstore held a contest asking "If M-O-A-B were an acronym, what would it stand for?" Responses poured in. Among them were these inspired answers:

Massive Outdoor Adventure Beckons

Multitude Of Awesome Blessings

Merriment Overcomes All Boundaries

Behind the Rocks: beyond Moab Rim, en route to Hidden Valley

Majesty Of Artistic Brilliance

Mystical Outpost of Ancient Beauty

Mindful Of All Beings

Mecca Of Audacious Backpackers

Mostly Outdoor Adoring Bodies

Marvelous Offerings Abound Benevolently

Read our favorite on page 88.

Want to voice your thoughts on the mysteries of this high-desert realm? Post them at www.hikingcamping.com. Click on "Guidebooks," "Hiking," then "Utah Canyon Country." Choose "Done in a Day: Moab" or "Hiking from Here to WOW: Utah Canyon Country." For either book, click on "Field Reports" and start typing.

Moab, in Spanish Valley

A Spectacular Collision

Moab isn't just a town. It's a spectacular collision.

Mormons, atheists, earth worshippers. Hikers, mountain bikers, four wheelers. Hippies, rednecks, tourists. Miners, artists, ranchers. All have collided here.

They're retired, they're young and wildly adventurous, they work nine-to-five. They live in trailer parks, gated communities, ranch-style homes, and Santa Fe adobe mansions. They drink wheatgrass juice, Pabst Blue Ribbon, whole milk, pinot noir. In their free time they rock climb, ride ATVs and hunt elk, read *The New Yorker*, volunteer at the local food bank.

Most settlements of this size—a mere 5,000 residents—tend to be comfortably, safely homogenous. Big cities accommodate diversity. Small towns not so much. And Moabites have keen, often conflicting interests in the surrounding desert: income vs. recreation, development vs. preservation, beauty vs. utility. Many have staked not only their livelihoods, but their very identity, in this stark land.

Yet Moab is not overtly contentious. Quite the opposite. The atmosphere is seductively harmonious. The disparate elements seem to have coalesced and are generally amicable.

There's conflict, of course. But less now than there once was, perhaps because prosperity is a pacifier. If most people have enough money—which these days arrives by the RV-load—it's easier to shrug off differences.

The tension remaining is probably good. Whether in a novel or a town, tension is what drives the plot, keeps it interesting. And Moab is definitely interesting. Rarely have so few people created such a yeasty brew, as evidenced by the town's long list of annual events. Here's a sampling:

Annual Skinny Tire Festival / early March / four days of organized rides for road cyclists / www.skinnytirefestival.com

Moab MUni Fest / late March / three days of mountain unicycling events / www.moabmunifest.com

Jeep Safari / mid March / nine days of 4WD trail rides / www.rr4w.com

April Action Car Show / late April / hot rods, muscle cars, classics & more / www.moab-utah.com/aprilaction

Moab Arts Festival / late May / jewelry, pottery, sculpture, clothing, photography & more / www.moabartsfestival.org

Moab Iron Horse Rally / late August / three days of motorcycle events / www.moabironhorse.com.

Moab Music Festival / September / classical, traditional, vocal & jazz performances, indoors & out / www.moabmusicfest.org.

Main Street, Moab

Labor Day Red Rock 4 Wheelers Campout / early September / overnight backcountry trips / www.rr4w.com

Skydive Moab Festival / late September / 3000 jumps in four days / www.skydivemoab.com

Moab Century Tour / early October / 100-mile road-cycling ride from canyons to mountains / www.skinnytirefestival.com

Gem & Mineral Show / mid October / lapidary exhibits, jewelry displays, field trips / www.moabrockclub.com

24 Hours of Moab Mountain Bike Race / mid October / team relay / www.grannygear.com

Moab Folk Music Festival / early November / local, regional & national performers, indoors & out / www.moabfolkfestival.com

As with any collision, observers' descriptions of Moab often don't jive. It's a matter of perspective. Some see cyclists and hikers who are in town only to grab an espresso for the drive to the trailhead. Others see an artists' colony where Main

Street is crowded with southwest-inspired creations ranging from totemic metalwork to hand-painted lampshades. But astute observers recognize that all Moabites, despite their polar differences, share a commendable trait: resilience.

The weather here is beyond harsh. It's sadistic, battering the town with incessant, muscular wind, searing it with branding-iron heat, leaving it parched and thirsty, then clobbering it with a bon-voyage-Noah! deluge that erodes but fails to slake. The economic climate—boom, bust, boom, bust—is equally fickle and punishing.

So everyone who rightfully calls Moab "home" is a tenacious survivor. They deserve to feel the esprit de corps of a battle-hardened combat platoon. They're certainly marching forward together on one front: pursuit of the most ambitious green-energy policies of any town in the American West.

Moab city government offices derive half their kilowatt-hours from emissions-free wind power. So do more than 15 percent of residents and 40 percent of businesses. As a result, the Environmental Protection Agency named Moab its first *Green Power Community*. But Moabites didn't take a bow and stop there.

They constructed a new city hall: geothermally heated and cooled. Moab Chevron became the first gas station in southern Utah to install biodiesel tanks and dispense the alternative fuel. Moab Cyclery powers its store with an eight-megawatt solar-electric system and runs five 15-passenger vans on used veggie oil. The River Canyon Lodge (www.rivercanyonlodge.com) participates in Utah Power's *Blue Sky* wind-power program.

For a collision, Moab is surprisingly admirable.

Après-Tromp

Moab has been mainlining tourism for many years. It needs you. But so thoroughly has the town mastered the art of wooing visitors, you'll likely feel the opposite: that you need it. Expect to feel an irresistible attraction to the ads posted in the local real-estate office windows while savoring Moab's abundant post-hike pleasures.

Riverside swimming pool at Sorrel River Ranch

The Moab Information Center, at the corner of Main and Center streets, is a fountain of knowledge. The Moab Area Travel Council distributes a booklet titled the *Moab Activities Planner* that other American cities would be wise to imitate. Tastefully designed and easy to read, it presents all the necessary facts without the typical marketing hype that assumes visitor = rube. Their excellent website (www.discovermoab.com) invites you to request a free copy.

What the *Moab Activities Planner* doesn't do—because it's obliged to be unbiased—is offer opinionated commentary that can save you time by directing your attention. So here you go: our advice on where to stay, where to eat, and where to experience the essence of Moab.

If you'd rather buy a new Osprey Atmos daypack than stay at a luxe hotel, but you want more of your lodging than simply a place to lay your head, make reservations at the **Cali Cochitta Bed & Breakfast Inn** (110 South 200 East Moab, 435-259-4961, toll free 888-429-8112, www.moabdreaminn.com). It's a late 1800s Victorian home, restored and renovated to its original classic style.

Cali Cochitta innkeepers Kim and David Boger routinely receive gushing thank-you notes. They have three large guest rooms, one suite, and one cottage. All are immaculate and sumptuous. Each has a queen bed, private bath, cable TV, and WiFi. The breakfast isn't a paltry "continental" affair. It's a lavish, fuel-you-all-day meal: hot entree, homemade muffins, fresh squeezed juices, and fresh seasonal berries with whipped cream and Grand Marnier sauce.

At the distant end of the lodging spectrum—several miles (literally and figuratively) beyond any Moab hotel—is **Sorrel River Ranch**. Stay here if you want to be as impressed by your room, the service, the food, and the property, as you are by the grandeur of the high desert. It's the only Small Luxury Hotel (www.slh.com) in Utah and the only AAA Four-Diamond resort in Moab.

Sorrel River Ranch on the Colorado River
Courtesy of Sorrel River Ranch

One of the shops on Main Street

The Sorrel setting is as picturesque as any on earth: a sweeping bend of the Colorado River, surrounded by dramatic canyon country à la Gene Autry, Louis L'Amour, or John Wayne. And the resort lives up to it. So much so, it's easy to limit your exploration to gazing. But that would be contrary to proprietor Robbie Levin's intent. He created Sorrel as a sybaritic base from which to explore the red-rock wilds beyond.

So get out there, then come back to dinner at the Sorrel River Grill, which serves American ranch classics with French fusion flair. Afterward, retire to your palatial suite with a vaulted, log-beam ceiling, hardwood floor, overstuffed sofa, and hydrotherapy clawfoot bathtub. Then step onto the private, riverside deck and enjoy the most precious luxury of all: tranquility.

Sorrel River Ranch (435-259-4642, toll free 877-359-2715, www. sorrelriver.com) is just east of mile marker 17 on Highway 128, about 20 minutes from Moab.

Somewhere between Cali Cochitta and Sorrel, literally in a canyon of its own, is a unique rental property: **Los Vados House** (www.losvados.com, 801-532-2651). It's an absolutely private, two-bed, two-bath home next to a year-round creek, about 15 miles from Moab. Rent it, and it's all yours. Only one other home—a mile distant—occupies the seven-acre retreat. To get there (the owners reveal the precise location only to guests) you must pass through two locked ranch gates and cross the creek, which requires a high-clearance, 4WD vehicle. If you don't want to mire the family sedan, the Los Vados caretaker will shuttle you. Designed by a San Francisco architect, built in 1998, Los Vados offers aristocratic comfort in a lonely, natural, scenic setting that elsewhere would necessitate carrying a backpack and pitching a tent.

After arriving in Moab and establishing your temporary residence, you're probably in need of refreshment. In the desert, simply standing still is thirsty work. If you're here to hike, staying hydrated is mission critical.

Your body craves pure water, so that's what you should be sipping all day. But for a celebratory guzzle, head for **Hogi Yogi** (396 South Main, 435-259-2656) or **Peace Tree Juice Cafe** (20 South Main, 435-259-8503). Hogi serves big, frosty, fruit smoothies. Peace whips up smoothies, too, but will also pour you a tall, ice-cold glass of vegetable or wheatgrass juice.

For hiking fuel, **City Market** (425 S Main, 435-259-5181) stocks a spectacular variety of energy bars. You can also stuff your daypack with power foods at nearby **Gear Heads** (471 South Main, 435-259-4327), an impressively serious outdoor shop that stays open late and offers free filtered water. Bring your own containers and load up: no limit, no purchase necessary. The record? A scout troop from Texas once marched out with 192 gallons.

Want to make your own hiking feast? Visit the **Moonflower Market** (39 East 100 North, 435-259-5712). It's more than a natural foods store. It's the counterculture vortex of Moab. You can learn a lot about the town just by stepping into the foyer and perusing the bulletin board.

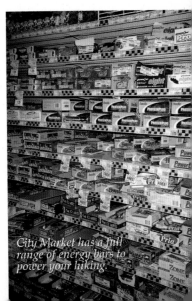

City Market has a full range of energy bars to power your hiking.

For breakfast, we recommend the one restaurant that serves nothing but breakfast: the **Jailhouse Cafe** (101 North Main, (435-259-3900). "Good enough for a last meal" is their motto, and they deliver on it. The line is sometimes so long, however, it appears you'll die of hunger. But hang in there, it's worth the wait. The menu includes ginger pancakes with Dutch apple butter, and eggs benedict with spicy southwest hollandaise sauce. Specials range from a smoked salmon omelet topped with chipotle sour cream, to French toast drizzled with warm peaches or raspberries. The restaurant's adobe-walled storage room was once the town jail, hence the name.

If your day doesn't start until you've topped up your caffeine level, swing into the **Wicked Brew Drive Thru** (132 North Main, 435-259-0021) for a Shot-in-the-Dark (coffee and double espresso). Or let **Moab's Daily Grind** (1146 South Hwy 191 #B 259-1115) boost your r.p.m. with a latte, mocha, cappuccino, or chai.

For a hormone-free yet manly burger, a heap of fresh-cut fries, and a genuine 1950s chocolate malt—all so reasonably priced you'll think it's a mistake—head for **Milt's Stop & Eat** (356 Millcreek Drive, 435-259-7424). This classic diner began serving uranium miners more than half a century ago and is still thriving today. Each item on the menu has a legion of local devotees, but the favorite is Milt's made-fresh-daily, whole-pinto-bean chili con carne. It's sure to power you— ka-boom!—a long way up the trail.

Even if you didn't pack your pearls or a necktie, you'll feel like you're wearing them when you dine at the **Center Cafe** (60 North 100 West, 435-259-4295), which serves the most sophisticated cuisine in town. Show up in Chaco sandals and Patagonia Baggies, if you like. No one will notice. They'll be contemplating the globally-inspired menu, admiring the superb service, or swooning over their meal.

As is often true of great restaurants, the owners of the Center Cafe are the head chefs: Zee and Paul McCarroll. The couple met at the Western Culinary Institute in Portland, Oregon, where they honed their complementary cooking styles and discovered a shared love of mountain biking. They often dashed to Moab to ride slickrock. But after settling here, their prowess in the kitchen curtailed their freedom. The business blossomed and cycling time shriveled.

The McCarroll's creations range from classic American, to Asian, to classic French. Their menu evolves to accommodate fresh, local, organic produce, seasonal foods, and their bountiful imaginations. Peruse their current fare at www. centercafemoab.com if you like, but it's not necessary. Just make a reservation. There are three things you can't leave Moab without doing. One is indulging your palate at the Center Cafe.

The second is **riding a mountain bike on slickrock**. Admittedly, it's frustrating for a hiker to see how marginalized hiking is in Moab. Biking gets all the attention here, despite the fact that only on foot can you fully explore and appreciate canyon country. It's also true, however, that biking on slickrock will instantly put a 1,000-watt grin on your face. And it's not just that sexy machine between your legs. It's what it enables you to do: spar with gravity.

The Shafer Trail (popular with 4WDers and mountain bikers) dives off Island in the Sky.

What most novices and even many advanced riders from elsewhere don't realize is that the desert isn't nearly so tough as the word "slick*rock*" implies. This is a fragile environment: easily, irrevocably damaged. To avoid being a destructive idiot and ensure you safely get maximum enjoyment from your ride, book a guided day tour with Dreamride (124 West 200 South, 435-259-6419, toll free 1-888-662-2882, www.dreamride.com). They rent superior bikes, employ expert guides, and promise you the ideal introduction to Moab mountain biking.

The third thing you can't leave Moab without doing is **wander down Main Street**. Many of the stores represent artists, artisans and craftspeople whose creativity is rooted in the town's American southwest provenance. You'll find it a stimulating couple hours, and you'll likely see something you want to take home—a beautiful reminder of how canyon-country touched you.

Our favorite shops are…

Earth Studio (31 North Main, 435-259-6445, toll free 800-463-4064, www.earthstudiomoab.com) specializes in metal art—whimsical, elegant, distinctive—for your home or garden.

Tom Till Gallery (61 North Main, 435-259-9808, www.tomtill.com) presents the stunning visual art of a long-time Moab resident who ranks among the world's most published photographers. The gallery sells affordable photo cards in addition to huge, framed prints.

Lema's Kokopelli Gallery (70 North Main, 435-259-5055, www.lematrading.com) sells jewelry, stoneware, pottery, rugs, and authentic Native American art.

Pinyon Tree Gift Shop (82 S. Main, 435-719-2086) stocks an array of southwest-inspired whatnots—amusing, useful, lovely, or all of the above.

Arches Book Company (78 North Main, 435-259-0782, http://arches.booksense.com) is an independent bookstore offering an eclectic mélange of literature, biography, natural history,

Frequently turn around and note prominent landmarks, so you're always oriented. Stay within your comfort zone. If you get anxious about finding your way back, it's time to head home. No one expects you to graduate from Sacajawea* University during a single afternoon of wandering.

You insist on a destination? Oh, alright. Aim for Gold Bar Arch. It has an uncanny resemblance to a 4WD vehicle, so it's also known as *Jeep Arch*. Roughly, here's how to find it.

Above the three pouroffs, ascend left. Near the first bay on the canyon's northwest wall, pick up a cairned, bootbeaten path. Scan ahead (left / north-northwest) for a spire in a saddle. Ascend to the base of the spire. Continue northwest on flatter terrain toward the next pass. Five minutes beyond the spire, the arch is visible right, in a southwest-facing wall. Five minutes farther, you'll be directly across from it, at 1.6 mi (2.6 km), 4887 ft (1490 m), about an hour from the trailhead.

*Sacajawea was the Shoshone woman who assisted Meriwether Lewis and William Clark while they explored western North America.

Moab Rim

Ascending slickrock slabs and ramps can be a giddy experience. Here's where to do it near Moab. The route immediately overlooks the Colorado River and quickly leads to grand views of the town, Spanish Valley, the Moab Rim, and *Behind The Rocks*—an intriguing chaos of sandstone fins, walls and domes.

4WD use precludes this from the Premier list. Think of the mechanized beasts as a curiosity rather than an annoyance, however, and you might be entertained. What those motorheads do in their rock crawlers *is* amazing.

It's possible to make this a 6.8-mi (10.9-km) one-way trip: exiting via Hidden Valley, ending near Hwy 191 southeast of Moab. But we recommend a 5-mi (8.1-km) round trip gaining about

Moab Rim trail above the Colorado River

1400 ft (427 m), so you spend most of your hiking time (about 2½ hours) on slickrock.

From the junction of Main (Hwy 191) and Center streets in Moab, drive south on Main 0.6 mi (1 km). At McDonald's, turn right (north) onto Kane Creek Blvd. Bear left at 1.4 mi (2.2 km). Reach the trailhead parking lot, on the left, at 3.2 mi (5.2 km), 4030 ft (1228 m).

Pass the huge, split boulder and ascend generally northeast on ramps of Kayenta sandstone. Unfortunately, white painted rectangles, brown plastic BLM posts, tire marks, and oil stains indicate the way.

Crest the rim at 1.1 mi (1.8 km), 4970 ft (1515 m). Gradually curve right (south) between Navajo sandstone domes. In 50 minutes, reach a signed fork at 1.8 mi (2.9 km), 4855 ft (1480 m). Go right (southwest)—the higher, scenic route. Soon curve southeast and ascend a slickrock dome. Top out at 2.5 mi (4 km), 4936 ft (1505 m), about 1¼ hours from the trailhead. Return the way you came.

Mill Creek Canyon

A perennial stream in a desert canyon is cause for celebration. This one is conveniently located on the edge of Moab, between soaring Navajo-sandstone walls harboring some exceptional prehistoric rock art. Cascades and swimming holes heighten its appeal.

But those attributes ensure you won't find solitude in the lower reaches of Mill Creek Canyon. You might find a crowd. You're certain to hear noise from Hwy 191 a half hour or more beyond the trailhead.

The consensus seems to be this isn't a serious hike. It's a place to cool off and relax, splash along in your Tevas, eat a big, fat burrito, stretch out on a comfy ledge, and bask in the sun. We agree. So instead of enshrining Mill Creek Canyon among our top ten trails, we're simply giving it an honorable mention.

Though very easy, an 8-mi (12.9-km), 5-hour round trip gaining about 300 ft (91 m) up Mill Creek's north fork to the confluence with Rill Creek Canyon would be exceptionally ambitious compared to most people's indolent agendas.

Mill Creek Canyon

Nearly everyone turns around well before, yet it's possible to go much farther.

The creek can be ankle- to knee-deep, and you'll be fording repeatedly, so amphibious footwear is preferable. Technical sandals designed for hiking are ideal. Fabric hiking boots you don't mind dunking are fine, too. A pack towel is also a good idea—to dry off at rest stops, or in case you swim.

From the Moab Information Center, at the corner of Main and Center streets, drive east on Center. In four blocks, turn right (south) onto 400 East. At Dave's Corner Market, turn left onto Millcreek Drive. Turn right at the stop sign. Take the next left (east) onto Powerhouse Lane and continue to the unpaved, trailhead parking lot at road's end. Elevation: 4429 ft (1350 m).

Before setting out, look upcanyon (east) from the parking lot. A shallow, eye-shaped alcove is visible near where the canyon's north and south forks split. You'll find rock art in the corners of that high alcove.

Begin hiking east on an old road. Pass a weir—the remains of a 1950s electricity-generating dam that was immediately KO'd by a silt-laden flashflood. Proceed on trail. In about ten minutes, bear left (east) to probe the steeper-walled north fork of Mill Creek Canyon. Right (south-southeast) is the south fork.

Following the path of least resistance—briefly in the water, often on a bootbeaten trail through brush, occasionally on ledges—work your way upstream along the canyon floor. Within 40 minutes of leaving the trailhead, stop to inspect the rock-art gallery in the large alcove on the left (north) wall.

About 50 minutes from the trailhead, reach a large pool. Backtrack five minutes to find the easy bypass route on the left (north) wall. After ascending, return to the canyon floor and resume on trail.

After hiking about 2½ hours, reach the confluence of Rill and Mill creeks at 4 mi (6.4 km), 4730 ft (1442 m). Rill is left (northeast). Mill Creek's north fork continues right (east-southeast). Rill has only a seasonal stream. This is the logical turnaround point for most hikers.

Probing Mill Creek Canyon

Taming Godzilla

The essence of hiking is appreciation of nature. As humanity's footprint on earth continues to grow, there's less nature for hikers to appreciate. That's especially true in the red-rock canyon country of southeast Utah, where humanity's footprint increasingly resembles Godzilla's.

The custodian for most of Utah's public land is the Bureau of Land Management (BLM), an agency within the United States Department of the Interior. The BLM is currently deciding which canyon-country areas should be preserved in their natural state, and which should be open to energy exploration and off-road vehicle (ORV) recreation. As of this writing, the BLM intends to sacrifice nearly two million acres of wilderness-quality land to ORV use.

You can influence the BLM, if you act now. Start by visiting the websites of the three conservation groups leading the effort to protect the fragile beauty of this spectacular region.

The Southern Utah Wilderness Alliance is the most effective group working to cure the BLM of myopia. SUWA's goal is not to ban ORVs but to simply reduce the amount of land that ORVs can legally rampage. Visit www.suwa.org to quickly voice your opinion to state officials.

Visit www.redrockheritage.org to see photos of rampaged canyon country. The website represents the Redrock Heritage Coalition, a group of southeast Utah residents and organizations who created the *Redrock Heritage Plan for Sustainable Economies and Ecosystems.*

The Redrock Heritage Plan is not an extremist proposal. It acknowledges ORV recreation as well as mountain biking and hiking. But it would restrict ORVs to designated roads and trails, because the majority of canyon-country visitors prefer to hike—in tranquility.

The plan also contends (and most geologists agree) that if all the undeveloped land in Utah were pierced with oil wells,

Behind the Rocks, beyond Moab Rim

it would extend the nation's oil supply by only three weeks and the natural gas supply by only five months, therefore oil and gas exploration in canyon country should be limited to existing, productive areas.

SUWA and the Redrock Heritage Coalition have a powerful ally: the Sierra Club. *America's Wild Legacy Initiative* is their effort to protect at least one exceptional wild place in every state within ten years. In Florida, it's the Everglades. In Alaska, it's the Arctic. In Utah, it's redrock canyon country. Visit www.sierraclub.org/wildlegacy/52places/ to learn more.

Ghosts In The Fog

Most accounts of Moab-area human history are brazenly ethnocentric. They make a vague, passing reference to the first people to wrest a living from this harsh land, then describe in tedious detail the relatively recent arrival of Spanish explorers (1765) and Mormon settlers (1855).

But the Paleo-Indians were here long before: roughly 14,000 years ago. And given that they roamed the region for millennia, they're the protagonists of the story. Everyone else is just a bit player.

The lack of hard information about Paleo-Indians, however, is exasperating. They're little more than ghosts in the fog. Archaeologists have nevertheless learned enough to provide us with a profile. It's only educated conjecture, much like a police artist's sketch of a suspect, but it's fascinating.

The Paleo-Indians were nomadic. Traveling on foot, carrying only a few meager possessions, they were the original ultralight backpackers. Along with their extended family—grandparents, siblings, children—they followed the seasons, always in search of food.

They wore clothing made of pelts and plant fibers. They slept in the open, took shelter in caves and canyon alcoves, or built rudimentary shelters out of brush and animal hide.

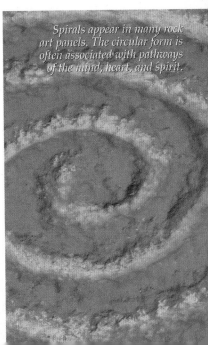

Spirals appear in many rock art panels. The circular form is often associated with pathways of the mind, heart, and spirit.

For ages, they persevered with no knowledge of how to use spearpoints for hunting. They foraged constantly, harvesting roots, seeds, fruit—whatever was edible. They cooked, but much of their diet was raw food, including larvae and insects.

Often they trapped or clubbed small game. They targeted newborn, injured, sick, and old animals, or scared away predators from fresh kills. Working together, they might have driven big-game herds over cliffs, slaughtering numerous animals at once.

By chipping stone into desired shapes, a process now known as "flint knapping," they made tools for cutting, scraping, hammering and chopping. They also made implements out of animal bones, horns or tusks, used smooth rocks to grind seeds into flour, and fashioned rudimentary equipment from plant fibers and wood.

When the Paleo-Indians began hunting with stone-pointed spears, it transformed their culture. Hunting big game (such as the wooly mammoth whose jawbone was found by paleontologists in Arches National Park) displaced foraging as their primary means of survival.

The more they hunted, the more skilled they became at flint knapping. Today, spear points are their culture's signature artifact and are considered the most beautifully crafted stonework from all of American prehistory.

Paleo-Indian hunters threw their spears, used them as lances, or propelled them with an "atlatl" or throwing stick. They probably hid near water sources and waited for their prey to arrive. Their first spear strike was unlikely to have killed, say a mastodon, so they must have continued chasing the injured animal—for miles or even days—inflicting wounds until it collapsed.

Attacking a mammoth or mastodon with a spear makes bullfighting look a lawn game. The potential reward, however, was immense: a feast for the entire clan, plus leftovers galore. A successful hunt must have incited an orgiastic celebration. Afterward, they'd strip the carcass. Meat, skin, ivory, bone, sinew—all were precious resources. They wasted nothing, because survival was always tenuous.

Archaeological evidence suggests Paleo-Indians did not wander aimlessly but traveled in annual circuits, following big game, seeking edible plants, mindful of the need for winter shelter. They traded and intermarried with other bands. The continent-wide distribution of similar spearpoints suggests a vast communication reach. But their precise migration vector to the present-day U.S. and into the desert southwest is unknown.

And that's just one of many questions that will remain unanswered. Who were these people, really? What kind of spirituality did they practice? What were their rituals? Did they make music? Dance? How were their small, mobile societies structured? What kind of language did they speak? The Paleo-Indians are an enigma. And a blurry one at that.

The Ancestral Puebloans

By the end of the Ice Age, the earth's vegetation had changed dramatically and many big-game species were extinct. So the descendants of the Paleo-Indians—the Desert Archaic Indians—adapted to a new world. They evolved from nomads to villagers, from hunter-gatherers to farmers.

It was a slow, primitive, agricultural renaissance. They formed larger bands and diversified culturally. Possibly influenced by the great Mayan civilization farther south, they created permanent settlements. Seeking more durable housing, they built pit houses (semi-subterranean lodges). They devised more complex tools, wove plant-fiber mats and baskets, made simple ceramics. And they developed new religious ideas, which they documented by painting and chiseling stone surfaces.

They built their pit houses on escarpments, knolls or mesas above drainages and arable land. Within each hamlet, they built a larger pit house for community meetings and ceremonies.

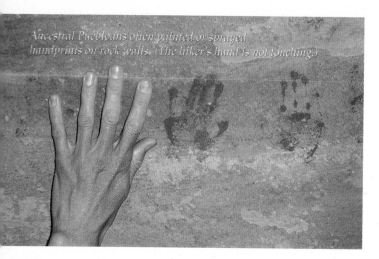

Ancestral Puebloans often painted or sprayed handprints on rock walls. (The hiker's hand is not touching.)

They created beautiful, delicate pottery and sophisticated, ornate baskets. They cached surplus food for lean times. They began hunting—and fighting—with bows and arrows. And they were the first people in all of what is now the southwest U.S. and northern Mexico to rely more on crops (corn, beans, squash) than on hunting and gathering.

Their cultural evolution into the Ancestral Puebloans around 1200 B.C. was marked by the abandonment of pit houses in favor of contiguous and multistory stone-and-mortar structures built atop the ground but usually sheltered by canyon walls.

The Puebloan population surged after 700 A.D. They spread into less hospitable areas, planted larger fields, developed complex irrigation systems, and became master craftsmen. They celebrated rituals by drumming, chanting and dancing in their community plazas and kivas (underground ceremonial chambers). Their civilization flourished between 900 A.D. and and 1130 A.D., then rapidly declined. A decades-long drought killed many of them and diminished resources so severely that survivors were constantly at war. It wasn't the scenery that inspired them to build fortress-like cliff dwellings; they were defending themselves from marauders.

Ancestral Puebloan dwellings

Though the Puebloans seem to have simply vanished around 1240 A.D., archaeologists believe those who survived the drought and escaped conflict did so by abandoning southeast Utah (in fact all of the Colorado Plateau, as well as southern New Mexico, southern Arizona, and northern Chihuahua) and migrating to other, more stable Native societies in west central New Mexico, northeast Arizona, and the upper Rio Grande River drainage.

Because the arid climate is gentle on archaeological sites, an astonishing number of Puebloan dwellings, granaries and rock-art panels are still intact today, seemingly enshrined within the canyons. This abundance of readily-visible cultural remains lends intellectual and spiritual stimulation to the experience of hiking in southeast Utah.

Bibles, Bombs, Boom & Bust

After the Ancestral Puebloans abandoned southeast Utah, various Native tribes succeeded them: Navajos, Hopis, but primarily the Utes. Spanish explorers arrived in the late 1700s, including an expedition led by Juan Maria Antonio de Rivera in 1765.

Traders and fur trappers established a route called the *Spanish Trail*, linking Taos and Santa Fe with southern California missions. It crossed the Colorado River immediately north of present-day Moab, where the Highway 191 bridge now stands. It was frequently traveled by 1830.

In 1855 the Mormon Church in Salt Lake City took an interest in the Moab area, then known as *Spanish Valley*. They sent a contingent to build a fort there, which the Native inhabitants rightfully saw as an aggressive invasion. A confusing, unplanned battle soon erupted. A few of the Mormons were killed. The rest departed the valley.

Natives once again had the region largely to themselves, but only for about two decades. Mormon settlers returned in 1878.

Pioneer home

They built a school and church in 1881 and, soon after, a ferry across the Colorado River. Their farms and cattle ranches were thriving by 1885. Completion of the railway between Denver and Salt Lake spurred growth because it brought the train within 35 miles of the settlement.

The Mormons called their town "Moab." According to the Bible, where the name appears 137 times, it was a lush valley in the desert, just shy of the Promised Land. According to the Mormon settlers, that was an accurate description of their new home, so they dubbed themselves "Moabites." Grand County was established in 1890, Utah became the 45th state in 1896, and Moab was incorporated as a town in 1902.

By 1906, the local newspaper, the *Grand Valley Times*, was promoting Moab's potential as a tourist destination. In 1909, the Moab Commercial Club was formed to advertise the area's scenic and recreational attractions.

A bridge finally spanned the Colorado River at Moab in 1912. By then orchards were well established, and the town was renowned for its fruit, particularly peaches. Meanwhile another industry—less benign but more profitable—gained momentum: mining.

Southeast Utah had produced $2.4 million worth of uranium by 1920. This initial boom fizzled when vast sources of the mineral were discovered elsewhere in the world. The regional mining industry continued growing, however, due to an abundance of potash (used in fertilizers), manganese and vanadium (both used in steel production), natural gas, and petroleum.

In 1929, President Hoover established Arches as a national monument. This event was the first pillar of the tourism industry Moab would eventually build and depend on, but if the townspeople recognized its importance, they can be excused for soon forgetting it. During the 1950s, the Cold War nuclear arms race made uranium mining extremely profitable again.

A flash flood of speculators, prospectors, miners and workers swelled the town's population from 1,275 in 1950 to 4,682 in 1960. They built one of the nation's largest uranium processing mills. Moab, "Uranium Capital of the World," spawned new motels, cafes, stores, schools and businesses.

1964 was a pivotal year for Moab. Decreased demand for uranium forced the closure of the area's largest uranium mine, which laid off hundreds of employees. And President Johnson established Canyonlands National Park—an act that significantly advanced the local tourism industry.

The La Sal Mountains and Behind the Rocks, from Kane Springs Road

By the 1970s, it was apparent Moab's economy would be powered by tourists rather than nuclear energy. In 1971, President Nixon established Arches National Monument as a National Park. In 1975, the park attracted 313,000 visitors. Meanwhile, river rafting had gained popularity, and Moab's location beside the Colorado River made it an ideal base for river trips.

Uranium mining companies continued cutting back in the early 1980s. Moab's population decreased 23%, and unemployment increased to 15%. At the same time, hope pedaled into town on two wheels. Moab gained fame as the "Mountain Biking Capital of the World."

By the late 1980s, Moab was aggressively marketing itself as a tourist destination, not only to mountain bikers but also to 4WD enthusiasts who saw the region's seemingly endless network of mining exploration roads as a vast playground.

Uranium recycled from decommissioned Soviet warheads flooded the world market in the early 1990s. Simultaneously, nuclear power-plant construction virtually halted. The price of uranium tumbled, and the industry collapsed. But by then, Moab had switched fuels. Its economy was soon running on high-octane tourism.

Today, Moab has about 5,000 residents—slightly less than its 5,333 high in 1980, substantially more than the 3,971 it had in 1990. But Moab now feels bigger than ever, because it welcomes more than 1.6 million tourists each year. The primary attractions are, of course, the nearby national parks: 800,000 people visit Arches each year, 400,000 visit Canyonlands.

Though it appeared Moab's uranium industry was dead, it's now rising from the grave. Uranium supplies are low, because the Soviet-legacy supply was depleted. And demand is high, because Russia, India and China are building dozens of nuclear plants. Americans' interest in nuclear power is also resurging as fossil fuels fall from grace. So the price of uranium—also called U308, or yellowcake—is headed skyward, and uranium mines are reopening.

How this might affect Moab is impossible to predict. Moabites are wary of another boom-bust phase, and they're now cruising smoothly on tourism—an infinitely renewable resource. Besides, there's still a 10.5-million-ton uranium tailings site (a parting gift from the long-defunct Atlas Mine) on the edge of town, beside the Colorado River. It will eventually be moved, but for now it certainly doesn't inspire an "Oh boy, more uranium!" sentiment.

Regardless of how Moab evolves, evidence of its past will remain prominently visible. Images of Kokopelli (the long-haired, dancing, flute-playing, Native fertility god) are so ubiquitous you'd think it was the town logo. And Moab's street grid, like that of most Utah cities, is distinctly Mormon. The address "26 West 100 North" means 26 blocks west and 100 blocks north of the temple.

Eight-foot long snake petroglyph

Rock Art

Southeast Utah is an immense outdoor art gallery. Natives, beginning many thousands of years ago with the Desert Archaic Indians, frequently carved and painted rock surfaces. An astonishing number of these rock-art sites have survived the ravages of time and are still visible today.

Archaeologists believe petroglyphs and pictographs represented spiritual visions, chronicled significant events, served as signage for passersby (advice, warnings), or were clan symbols. Though these interpretations make sense, they're merely educated conjecture. We'll never know for sure what the artists intended. Perhaps they were simply amusing each other. It will remain a mystery, adding intrigue to the allure of canyon country.

Petroglyphs were carved (pecked, scratched, incised) *into* the rock. Pictographs were painted (using mineral pigments or plant dyes) on the rock surface. Most people get them mixed up. But you'll remember the difference if you know the terms' origins.

"Petro" comes from the Greek "petros," which means "stone," and "glyphein," which means "carve." So a petroglyph is carved in stone.

"Picto" comes from the Latin "pictus," which means "painted." "Graph" is of Greek origin and means "record." So a pictograph is a painted record.

Petroglyphs are usually on the dark-brown or black vertical streaks called *desert varnish* that stain most canyon walls. Pictographs are usually on the smooth sandstone of the Navajo (buff colored) and Wingate (reddish) formations. The Natives created most of their art within sheltering alcoves or beneath protective overhangs where rain wouldn't harm it.

Rock art is strewn throughout the Moab area. You don't even have to hike to see it. Many remarkable panels are visible from pavement, for example along Kane Creek Boulevard and the Potash Road. But two of the most arresting rock-art sites in the region are a short drive out of town.

One of many rock art panels beside Hwy 279 (Potash Road) at 5 mi (7.8 km)

You're heading north? Visit Sego Canyon, about 45 minutes from Moab. It's not far from the junction of Hwy 191 and Interstate 70. You're heading south? Visit Newspaper Rock—on Hwy 211, which accesses the Needles District of Canyonlands National Park.

When viewing rock art, resist the urge to touch it. The oil on your skin will speed the deterioration of the paint and even the sandstone itself. Put your hand on a petroglyph or pictograph and you're defacing it. Touching = vandalism. The damage, though not immediately visible, will be irrevocable and possibly severe.

The way to feel rock art is not with your hands but with your heart. Remind yourself that the artists were human beings very much like you. They had desires, fears, dreams. They felt joy, sorrow, pain. They could be emotional, logical, confused. They were smart, ignorant, curious. They worked hard and got lazy. They treasured life and dreaded death. They too were perplexed by the meaning of it all. With that in mind, perhaps you can begin to fathom what they were trying to say. Empathy, after all, is the first step toward understanding.

Sego Canyon

Rock-art panels up to 6,000 years old, from three Native American periods: Barrier Canyon, Fremont, and Ute.

The Barrier-style panel has ten nearly life-size anthropomorphic shapes. They're similar to those in the famous Grand Gallery, in Horseshoe Canyon (described in *Hiking From Here to WOW: Utah Canyon Country*, and at www.utah.com > national parks > canyonlands > horseshoe canyon). Heavy trapezoidal bodies appear to float in space. Many have long, curved horns or antennae, and round, enlarged, staring eyes. Some archaeologists believe the figures were created by shamans during or after trance states in which they contacted, or felt they had become, supernatural beings. Perhaps the drawings were an attempt to communicate to others what they'd experienced.

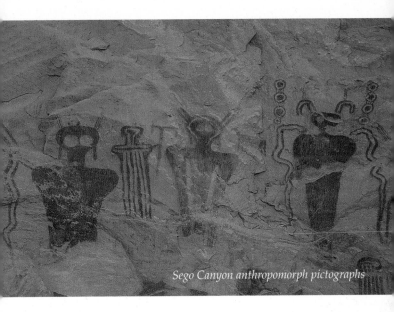

Sego Canyon anthropomorph pictographs

From Moab, drive Hwy 191 north-northwest 30 mi (48 km), turn right (east) onto I-70, then proceed 5 mi (8 km) to Exit 185. Continue north 3.5 mi (5.6 km)—through the ghost town of Thompson Springs, beyond the railroad tracks—to the parking lot on the left. A path leads 165 yd (150 m) to the rock-art site. Directly across the canyon are two more panels above a corral.

Newspaper Rock

A single, spectacular panel bearing some 2,000 years of rock art from the Fremont, Ancestral Puebloan, Navajo, and Anglo cultures.

In the Navajo language, the panel is called *Tse' Hane*, which means "rock that tells a story." Though you're unlikely to decipher a story no matter how long you stare, you will see hundreds of figures on this 8-by-20-ft (2.4-by-6.1-m) expanse of rock. They include paw prints, hooves, elk with huge antlers, a deer herd, a migration of animals, bighorn sheep, lizards, buffalo, snakes, various symbols, shamans, even a six-toed human foot.

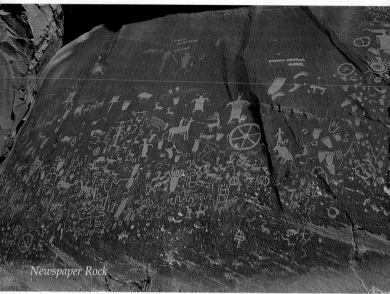
Newspaper Rock

From Moab, drive Hwy 191 south 38.5 mi (62 km). Turn right (west) onto Hwy 211, which is signed for Canyonlands National Park, Needles District. Continue another 12.3 mi (19.8 km) to the parking lot on the right.

Just 1.9 mi (3 km) farther is a pullout on the left (east). From there, if you walk across dry Indian Creek and continue 110 yd (100 m) to the cliffs at the Shay Canyon confluence, you'll find two more venerable but overlooked rock-art panels.

The Colorado Plateau

The map on the facing page shows the Colorado Plateau —130,000 sq mi (337,000 sq km) drained by the Colorado River and its major tributaries: the Green, San Juan, and Little Colorado rivers.

The Colorado Plateau is mostly sandstone, shale and limestone deposited in horizontal layers hundreds of millions of years ago. Much of it is deeply incised with countless canyons,

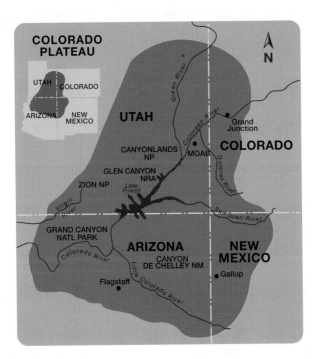

valleys, gorges, chasms, gulches and arroyos. Think of the surface of the human brain. From an aerial perspective, the plateau has a similar, marvelously complex appearance created by erosion (water, wind, ice) and weathering (decomposition).

This superficial chaos, however, belies one of the Colorado Plateau's distinguishing geologic traits. It's essentially a high, thick, crustal block where relatively little rock deformation (violent uplifting, faulting, folding) has occurred within the past 600 million years. Yet the surrounding regions were dramatically deformed. The Rocky Mountains (north and east) were thrust skyward, and tremendous, earth-stretching tension created the Basin and Range (west and south).

Most of the hiking trails in this book reveal a vertical cross-section of the Colorado Plateau. The visible rock strata represent the region's geologic history from about 300 to 65 million years ago. To appreciate what you're seeing, however, you don't need to understand it. Beauty is never enhanced by explanation.

Memorizing how "the compressional impetus of the Laramide orogeny downfolded the rocks between the salt anticlines into broad synclines and reactivated the basement faults" will, unless you're a geologist, eviscerate your canyon-country experience.

Still, you might find this strange land even more intriguing if you have a sense for the magnitude of the forces that created it. Or not. What follows is a brief summary, so you have the opportunity to at least be scantily informed.

Pennsylvanian Period – 325 to 300 million years ago

Much of Utah was covered by ocean. While the mountains rose to the east, the area around Moab subsided, forming a broad, deep sinkhole: the Paradox Basin.

Seawater was trapped in the basin and became increasingly saline due to evaporation. Fresh seawater sometimes refilled the basin but never flushed out the very salty water, in fact the new water floated above the brine.

After millions of years, the basin contained salt deposits up to 5000 ft (1520 m) thick. Potash (a salt potassium used to make fertilizer) is mined from this layer—the Paradox formation—near Moab.

Permian Period – 300 to 251 million years ago

The ocean retreated west, leaving the Paradox Basin dry. Lowland coastal sand dunes and marine sand bars dominated the Moab area. But severe erosion in the mountains to the east deposited alluvial fans of iron-rich red sandstone in the basin.

The dunes are the White Rim sandstone bench on which the White Rim Trail circles the Island in the Sky in Canyonlands National Park. (See Trip 7, Murphy Hogback.)

The alluvial fans are the Cutler formation: the layer of brick-red rock visible in the Needles district of the park. (See Trip 10, The Needles.)

Sandstone

Triassic Period – 251 to 200 million years ago

Southeast Utah was a huge, level floodplain, where the seashore advanced and receded over vast mudflats. With no steep gradients, the rivers were broad and slow. They deposited deep silt and sand.

During the lower (older) Triassic, the mudstone Moenkopi formation was created. Though it can be yellowish-gray or pale olive, it's often reddish brown or maroon, for example at Fisher Towers (Trip 3).

During the upper (more recent) Triassic, the Chinle formation was created. This layer also varies in color, but tends to be deep, dark purple or indigo. The Murphy Hogback trail (Trip 7), near its lowpoint, follows a wash through Chinle sandstone.

By the end of the Triassic, the sea was distant west, and the Moab area became a desert.

Desert varnish on Wingate sandstone

Jurassic Period – 200 to 145 million years ago

Sand dunes developed in the desert climate. They buried the floodplain and became the thick layer of reddish Wingate sandstone visible in the cliffs west of Moab and the spires of Castle Valley.

A period of wet weather then created streams that cut through the dunes, depositing the reddish-brown to lavender sandstone of the Kayenta formation. Mountain bikers ascend Kayenta ledges on both sides of the Portal (where the Colorado River pierces the Moab Rim.)

The harder Kayenta protects the underlying, softer Wingate from breakdown, allowing it to form cliffs up to 400 ft (122 m) high that extend long distances with few breaks, thus impeding travel.

When the arid climate resumed, it created a huge, Sahara-like desert across much of western North America. Deep sand dunes accumulated, forming the buff-colored Navajo sandstone.

Meanwhile, western Utah was rising in altitude and eastern Utah was dropping. Among the layers created in the resulting floodplain mudflats was the salmon-colored Entrada formation.

The major features in Arches National Park are Navajo and Entrada sandstone. It's easy to remember most of the arches are Entrada, because it's the Spanish word for "entrance."

Uranium and vanadium deposits, as well as dinosaur fossils and tracks, are primarily found in the Morrison formation, which occurred in the upper (more recent) Jurassic.

Cretaceous Period – 145 to 65 million years ago

What is now the Gulf of Mexico was much bigger. It covered the middle of North America including eastern Utah. Only near the end of the Cretaceous was the Moab area again above water.

When the Rocky Mountains rose, so did the Colorado Plateau, by thousands of feet (hundreds of meters), yet the strata remained generally horizontal. In other words it was still a plateau.

The Colorado River established a new course—its present one— slicing deep into the plateau en route to the Pacific Ocean.

Paleogene – 65 to 23 million years ago

The Paradox formation salt deposits were a mile deep. Intense pressure from the sedimentary layers above caused the salt to flow like a glacier. It shifted, buckled, liquefied, forced the earth above into domes, and collapsed into cavities.

Erosion stripped away the surface. Water seeped into cracks and froze. It split slabs into boulders, boulders into rocks, rocks into pebbles. Wind and rain swept away the debris. An array of free-standing fins remained. Further erosion and weathering destroyed many of the fins. In others it formed holes. Voilà: the celebrated arches.

The shifting salts also created the Moab Fault, prominently visible behind the Arches National Park entrance. The fault lines bracket present-day Moab. Geologists believe water seeped in

Ancient cottonwoods

and dissolved the salt layers below, causing the land to sink. The result is the Moab Valley, also called the Spanish Valley.

Neogene – 23 million years ago to present

Most of the canyon-cutting erosion that shaped the current topography of the Colorado Plateau happened as recently as five million years ago.

About two million years ago, during the last ice age, heavy precipitation quickened the pace of canyon-cutting. The Colorado and Green river canyons deepened and widened especially fast, because they were fed by glacial runoff from the Rocky Mountains.

Tough Hombres

To survive in the Utah desert, shrubs and trees have to be tough hombres—able to withstand long periods without water, willing to split rocks with their roots in search of nutrients.

They're generally small and far apart compared to trees and shrubs in moister climes. Here, the scarcity of water limits their size and requires them to disperse. But once established, they cling obstinately to life. They're certainly hardier than most humans. Many can thrive for a century or more.

The most prolific shrubs are Mormon tea, blackbrush, rabbitbrush, saltbush, cliffrose, sage, and greasewood. Prickly pear cactus is also common. Cottonwood and willow trees tend to grow where water is most abundant: primarily beside the watercourses on canyon and valley floors. That's also true of bamboo-like tamarisk and thorny Russian olive—aggressively invasive non-native tree species that rapidly colonize stream environments and make hiking a chore.

The predominate trees in southeast Utah are piñon pine and juniper. "P-J forests," as they're known to hikers, cover millions of acres at elevations between 4,500 ft (1372 m) and 7,000 ft (2134 m).

Juniper blue cones (berries)

Utah Juniper

Piñon pine

Piñons have crooked trunks, reddish bark, and grow very slowly. A 10-ft (3-m) specimen with a 4- to 6-in (10- to 15-cm) diameter trunk might be 80 to 100 years old. Their extensive root systems mirror the size of the above-ground tree. They produce compact cones bearing tasty pinenuts, which were a vital source of protein for Natives.

Junipers are the archetypal Utah desert tree. Their gnarled, twisting branches artfully illustrate the grasping, painful effort necessary to persevere in an inhospitable environment. During a drought, junipers will prevent fluids from flowing to their peripheral branches in order to live, hence their "half flourishing, half dead" appearance. Scale-covered leaves and bluish, waxy-coated seeds help the tree conserve moisture.

Rodentville

Knowing the facts, you might think the desert itself is a mirage. How could a couple hundred species of bird, 65 species of mammal, two dozen species of reptile, nearly a dozen species of amphibian, and eight species of—get this—fish (!) exist in such a desiccated, rock-hard land? Well, they do. So rub your eyes, shake your head, look again.

Specifically, look up. Birds are the most frequently visible canyon-country creatures. Even on the hottest summer days, turkey vultures and white-throated swifts circle above. In riparian corridors, particularly along the Colorado River, birdsong is audible most mornings. The musicians include blue grosbeaks, yellow-breasted chats, spotted towhees, and canyon wrens. Great blue herons hunt the shallows for fish. Cooper's hawks flit through the dense riverside brush.

Say's phoebes, black-throated sparrows, and western meadowlarks inhabit the desert grasslands. Piñon jays, scrub jays, juniper titmice, black-throated gray warblers, and owls frequent the P-J woodlands. And it's possible to see hawks, eagles and ravens almost anywhere.

Members of the crow family, ravens are jet black, intelligent, able to solve problems, playful, and communicative. No wonder they're prescient beings in Native folklore.

The one mammal you're certain to see in canyon country.

As for mammals, the desert favors small ones. Diminutive size is an adaptation to the harsh environment. Smaller creatures can find shelter easier and need less water and food. So southeast Utah is Rodentville. Mice and rats thrive here.

Among the most interesting desert rodents is the tiny kangaroo rat, which produces its own water by metabolizing plant matter—its only food source. It spends hot days sleeping in a cool burrow and might even plug the opening with dirt or debris for added insulation.

Because "rodent" has negative connotations, most people don't realize squirrels, chipmunks, porcupines and beaver are rodents too. All live in southeast Utah. So do skunks, which, despite their vaguely rodent-like appearance, are omnivores that help keep the desert rodent population in check. Bats are also common here but are not, as some people assume, "flying rodents." We once saw thousands of bats swoop en masse out of a crack in a canyon wall.

Other desert animals—many of which are "crepuscular" (most active at dawn and dusk) or strictly nocturnal—include cottontails, black-tailed jackrabbits, foxes, bobcats, mule deer, bighorn sheep, and mountain lions. It's rare for people to see a big cat. If you're lucky, you might see a paw print. But should you glimpse a herd of mule deer, you'll know a mountain lion is probably nearby, because deer are their primary food source.

Lizard

Though coyotes range throughout Central and North America, from Panama to Alaska, they're a classic desert animal. They tend to be nocturnal or crepuscular yet can also be "diurnal" (active by day) when necessary. They're omnivorous, but their chief food in southeast Utah is—hurray!—rodents.

Coyotes are wily, brave opportunists and masters of adaptability. You're as likely to see one trotting across Center Street in Moab as you are in a lonely canyon. Hearing their call-and-response yipping and howling in the desert night is a thrill. Like the raven, the coyote figures prominently in Native folklore. He's the "trickster" who scandalizes, disgusts, amuses, disrupts, chastises, or humiliates.

Reptiles, however, are the iconic desert creatures. Chances are good you'll encounter a western whiptail lizard (with a tail twice as long as its body) basking in the sun on a boulder. Or you might cross paths with a western collared lizard: bright green with a distinctive, dapper, black collar.

Though "desert = snakes" in most people's minds, snakes are nocturnal and therefore rarely seen. People also assume snakes are dangerous, yet most are harmless. All will escape from human confrontation given the opportunity.

A few snakes in southeast Utah, of course, are venomous, for example the midget-faded rattlesnake. So are scorpions and black-widow spiders. But because they hunt only at night and will have knocked off work and be kicking back in rock crevices or under ledges during the hours you'll likely be hiking, they pose little threat. Just watch where you step, and never put your hand on a surface you can't see.

Snakes and lizards power-down to a state of torpor during the winter, are active during the day in late spring and early fall, and are crepuscular during summer. Lizards store fat in their tails—for nourishment while they're sedentary in winter. So losing a tail, even though it can grow back, is a life-threatening crisis for a lizard.

If lizards and snakes, with their scaley skin and beady eyes, make you uneasy, remember: they're on your side with regard to controlling the desert rodent population.

It's Alive!

Moab is surrounded by a slickrock vastness that invites you to hike off trail, wander freely, explore at will. And as long as it's *rock* that's under foot, you can go wherever you want, as far as you like, limited only by your instinct for self preservation. But when hiking on other surfaces, there's more at stake than your own enjoyment and safety; there's the wellbeing of the desert ecosystem.

Nearly 75% of the Colorado Plateau's surface area is alive. It's covered by organisms that, though lowly in stature and humble in appearance, are critical to the survival of other desert flora, which in turn are vital to all desert fauna. These organisms are collectively known as *biological soil crust*.

They're also called *microphytic, microbiotic, cryptobiotic,* or *cryptogamic soil*. The most inclusive term is probably *biocrust*, which distinguishes it from physical or chemical crusts while not limiting the crust components to plants. But *cryptogam* is the name you'll hear most often. To keep it simple, we'll just call it *crypto*.

Cryptogamic soil

Crypto is composed of cyanobacteria, algae, mosses, lichens, liverworts, and fungi. On the Colorado Plateau, mature crypto is usually darker than the surrounding soil, often appears black, and can be 4 inches (10 cm) thick.

Crypto stabilizes sand and dirt, prevents erosion by water or wind, promotes moisture retention, and feeds nutrients to nearby vegetation. It even captures nitrogen from the air, converts it to a form necessary for plant growth, and assimilates it into the soil.

When wet, crypto swells and spreads, gradually creating a complex, protective, nurturing layer over the otherwise very vulnerable surface of the surrounding terrain. Without crypto, the desert would be less hospitable than it already is. Yet crypto itself is quite vulnerable. It's instantly pulverized by an errant hiker, mountain biker, or 4WD vehicle.

Each time your boot lands on a patch of crypto—crunch, crunch, crunch—you destroy it and thus jeopardize every living thing in the vicinity, all of which contribute to the beauty you came here to witness.

Crust trampled to dust can take up to 250 years to fully regenerate. Meanwhile, water runoff increases by up to 50% (think *flashflood*), soil loss increases by up to 600% (think *duststorm*), and windblown sand kills yet more crypto by burying it and preventing photosynthesis (think *Boston Strangler*).

Freeze! Step away from the crust!

Whenever you're not hiking on slickrock or established trail, be alert for crypto. Avoid it diligently. Go around. Rockhop. Opt for gravel or sand. Follow drainage paths (rivulets, washes) where crypto doesn't grow. If hiking with kids, summarize your crypto explanation with a rule they'll easily remember: "Don't bust the crust."

Stepping on a tuft of grass is preferable to stepping on crypto, because the grass will survive and rebound, the crypto won't. If you absolutely must walk on crypto, imagine it's your mother's grave. Get off asap. Minimize damage by telling companions to follow your precise steps, so your group doesn't rampage a broad swath.

Wilderness Ethics

We hope you're already conscientious about respecting nature and other people. If not, here's how to pay off some of your karmic debt load.

Let wildflowers live. They blossom for only a few fleeting weeks. Uprooting them doesn't enhance your enjoyment, and it prevents others from seeing them at all. We once heard parents urge a string of children to pick as many different-colored flowers as they could find. Great. Teach kids to entertain themselves by destroying nature, so the world continues marching toward environmental collapse.

Leave no trace. Be aware of your impact. Travel lightly on the land. After a rest stop, take a few minutes to look for and obscure any evidence of your stay. Restore the area to its natural state.

Pack out everything you bring. Never leave a scrap of trash anywhere. This includes toilet paper, nut shells, and cigarette butts. Fruit peels are also trash. They take years to decompose, and wild animals won't eat them. And don't just pack out *your* trash. Leave nothing behind, whether you brought it or not. Keep a small plastic bag handy, so picking up trash is easy.

Prickly pear cactus

Poop without impact. In the wilds, choose a site at least 60 m (66 yd) from trails and water sources.

Ground that receives sunlight part of the day is best. Use a trowel to dig a small cat hole—10 to 20 cm (4 to 8 inches) deep, 10 to 15 cm (4 to 6 inches) wide—in soft, dark, biologically active soil. Afterward, throw a handful of dirt into the hole, stir with a stick to speed decomposition, replace your diggings, then camouflage the site. Pack out used toilet paper in a plastic bag. You can drop the paper (not the plastic) in the next outhouse you pass. Always clean your hands with a moisturizing hand sanitizer, like Purell. Sold in drugstores, it comes in conveniently small, lightweight, plastic bottles.

Urinate off trail, well away from water sources. The salt in urine attracts animals. They'll defoliate urine-soaked vegetation, so aim for dirt or rock.

Respect the reverie of other hikers. On busy trails, don't feel it's necessary to communicate with everyone you pass. Most of us are seeking solitude, not a soiree. A simple greeting is sufficient to convey good will. Obviously, only you can judge what's appropriate at the time. But it's usually presumptuous and annoying to blurt out advice without being asked. "Boy, have you got a long way to go." "The views are much better up there." "Be careful, it gets rougher." If anyone wants to know, they'll ask. Some people are sly. They start by asking where you're going, so they can tell you all about it. Offer unsolicited information only to warn other hikers about conditions ahead that could seriously affect their trip.

Hiking with Your Dog

"Can I bring Max, my Pomeranian?" The answer depends on which trail you intend to hike:

1. Corona Arch **Yes**, but it's not recommended due to steep slickrock where hikers are aided by cables and a ladder.

2. Morning Glory Canyon **Yes**, but you should keep it leashed and stay on the established trail.

3. Fisher Towers **Yes**, but you should keep it leashed and stay on the established trail. There is one short ladder where you'd have to carry your dog.

4. Mary Jane Canyon **Yes**, but you should keep it leashed.

5. Big Spring & Squaw canyons **No**, due to national park regulations.

6. Devils Garden **No**, due to national park regulations.

7. Murphy Hogback **No**, due to national park regulations.

8. Peekaboo **No**, due to national park regulations.

9. Upheaval Dome **No**, due to national park regulations.

10. The Needles **No**, due to national park regulations.

Bringing your dog hiking with you, however, isn't simply a matter of "Can I or can't I?" The larger question is "Should I or shouldn't I?"

The desert is even less accommodating of dogs than it is of people. Paws are quickly abraded by slickrock and burned in scorching-hot sand. A dog's nose is vulnerable to prickly, thorny vegetation. Dogs are very susceptible to overheating and dehydration. Leave your dog in your vehicle, and it could die surprisingly fast.

In Canyonlands and Arches national parks, don't even consider leaving your dog unattended in the frontcountry so that you can go backcountry hiking. It's prohibited. They don't even allow you to leave it tethered or otherwise confined.

Most humane dog owners agree: do not take your dog into the desert. If your dog is with you in Moab, leave it at a kennel while you go hiking.

If you insist that your dog accompany you on the trail, keep it leashed at all times—for its own safety, out of respect for your fellow hikers, and to ensure your dog doesn't trample the fragile, biological soil crust.

Put protective booties on your dog's feet. Carry tweezers so you can remove spines and needles from its paws and nose. Carry lots of extra water and—so it doesn't go to waste—a bowl for your dog to drink from.

Maps

The following Trails Illustrated maps can be useful to hikers: *Moab North (500)*, *Moab South (501)*, *Arches National Park (211)*, and *Canyonlands National Park / Needles & Island in the Sky (210)*.

The maps we created and that accompany each trip in this book are for general orientation only. Our *On Foot* directions are elaborate and precise, so referring to a topo map shouldn't be necessary. Nevertheless, you might want one.

After reaching a revelatory viewpoint, a topo map will enable you to interpret the surrounding geography. If the terrain through which you're hiking intrigues you, a topo map can contribute to a more fulfilling experience.

The stats box for each trip indicates which *Trails Illustrated* map to bring. Visit www.maps.nationalgeographic.com to purchase them online. They're also available at the Moab Information Center and Gear Heads (immediately south of City Market).

Carry A Compass

Left and *right* are relative. Any hiking guidebook relying solely on these inadequate and potentially misleading terms should be shredded and dropped into a recycling bin.

You'll find all the *On Foot* descriptions in this book include frequent compass directions. That's the only way to accurately, reliably guide a hiker.

What about GPS? Compared to a compass, GPS units are heavier, bulkier, more fragile, more complex, more time consuming, occasionally foiled by vegetation or topography, dependent on batteries, and way more expensive.

Keep in mind that the compass directions provided in this book are of use only if you're carrying a compass. Granted, our route descriptions are so detailed, you'll rarely have to check your compass. But bring one anyway, just in case.

A compass is required hiking equipment—anytime, anywhere, regardless of your level of experience, or your familiarity with the terrain.

Clip your compass to the shoulder strap of your pack, so you can glance at it quickly and easily. Even if you never have to rely on your compass, occasionally checking it will strengthen your sense of direction—an enjoyable, helpful, and conceivably lifesaving asset.

Keep in mind that our stated compass directions are always in reference to true north. In Moab, that's approximately 11° left of (counterclockwise from) magnetic north. If that puzzles, you, read your compass owner's manual.

Physical Capability

Until you gain experience judging your physical capability and that of your companions, these guidelines might be helpful.

Anything longer than a 7-mi (11.3-km) round-trip dayhike can be taxing for someone who doesn't hike regularly. Trips 1, 2, 3, 4, and 5—the easiest trips in this book—are within that range

Moderately fit striders enjoy dayhiking 11 mi (17.7 km).

A 1500-ft (457-m) elevation gain in that distance is challenging but possible for anyone in average physical condition. Trips 6, 7, 8, 9, 10b, 10c, and 10d are reasonable options for intermediate hikers.

Strong outdoor athletes are comfortable hiking 15 mi (24.1 km) and ascending 3280 ft (1000 m)—or more—in a single day. Few canyon-country dayhikes and none in this book entail nearly so much elevation gain. But you'll be approaching that level of exertion if, on a warm day, you combine options a, b, and d for Trip 10.

Weather

	AVERAGE HIGH		AVERAGE LOW		AVERAGE RAIN		AVERAGE SNOW		SUNRISE & SUNSET	
	°F	°C	°F	°C	IN	CM	IN	CM	A.M.	P.M.
JANUARY	41	5	17	-8	.67	1.7	4.5	11.4	7:34	5:22
FEBRUARY	51	11	24	-4	.63	1.6	2	5.1	7:09	5:57
MARCH	61	16	32	0	.79	2	1	2.5	6:29	6:26
APRIL	72	22	40	4	.76	1.9	-	-	6:42	7:55
MAY	82	28	48	9	.7	1.8	-	-	6:06	8:23
JUNE	93	34	56	13	.3	.76	-	-	5:53	8:44
JULY	98	37	63	17	.8	2	-	-	6:06	8:42
AUGUST	96	36	60	16	.9	2.3	-	-	6:33	8:12
SEPTEMBER	87	31	51	11	.7	1.8	-	-	7:00	7:26
OCTOBER	73	23	39	4	1	3	-	-	7:28	6:40
NOVEMBER	56	13	27	-3	.65	1.7	.4	1	7:00	5:05
DECEMBER	44	7	20	-7	.8	.2	3.5	9	7:29	4:58

World Peace Panel, beside Hwy 279 (Potash Road) at 5 mi (7.8 km)

Flashfloods

A flashflood is possible any day of the year in the desert. A sudden, violent thunderstorm can—with alarming speed—send an ominous wall of water ripping through a canyon: uprooting trees, hurling boulders, sweeping hikers into a deadly maelstrom. Your chance of survival? Poor to nil.

The rain doesn't even have to fall nearby to be a threat. It's conceivable you wouldn't see the clouds, feel the rain, or hear the thunder associated with a storm that imperiled you. So always be alert for the possibility of a flashflood, regardless of how sunny it is in your immediate vicinity.

Check the weather report before hiking. Rain is likely? Alter your plans. Avoid canyons and washes, or simply don't hike. On the trail, even if the weather is fine, be observant. Watch the sky for signs of impending rain. Listen for a roar coming from upcanyon. Habitually ask yourself, "Where could I quickly escape to higher ground?"

If you're hiking in a canyon, and it starts to rain, don't continue. Assuming you'll recognize danger in time to avoid it could be your fatal mistake. Stop. Return to the trailhead. By the time you know a flash flood is imminent, you're at serious risk.

If the rain is heavy and the trailhead is too distant, seek elevation and shelter. Don't endanger yourself climbing unless you're obviously in a life-threatening emergency. Just carefully work your way upward until you're as high above the drainage floor as you feel safe ascending.

After two hours of rain, this canyon was flooding.

Try to gain about 30 to 40 ft (9 to 12 m). Ideally, find a perch beneath an overhanging ledge. But don't sacrifice elevation for shelter. Once you've reached safety, make yourself as comfortable as possible, then be patient.

Desert rainstorms, and the flashfloods they cause, tend to be shortlived. Wait until the rain stops and the water subsides before resuming your retreat to the trailhead. And don't risk getting lost by attempting an unfamiliar, cross-country return route. Stay put until you can exit via the same trail you entered.

Thermonuclear Protection

In summer, the desert heat will bake your enchilada. So don't hike here during June, July or August. It's miserable and unsafe.

Late spring and early fall can still be hot enough to steam your tortilla, so always take these precautions:

• Pack at least two quarts (liters) of water per person on a short dayhike, and at least three per person on a long dayhike. Limit yourself to pure, fresh H20. No pop, no juice, no alcohol. But adding electrolyte powder can help replenish what your body loses via perspiration.

- Wear sunglasses. Generously rub sunblock on all your exposed skin.

- In addition to shorts and a shortsleeve shirt, bring desert-rat clothes for when the sun is intense: a hat with a broad brim; an ultralight, longsleeve shirt; lightweight, long pants; and a bandana you can moisten and wrap around your neck.

- Be conservative when estimating the distance you intend to cover. Allow more time than you'll probably need.

- Before departing the trailhead, make sure you're completely hydrated. Leave several full water bottles in your vehicle for a post-hike guzzle.

- Start hiking early in the morning, while it's still cool.

- Sip water throughout the day to prevent dehydration. Eat snacks frequently. Rest more often than you think necessary—in shade whenever possible. Stop for a long, relaxing, nourishing lunch.

- Pace yourself. If you feel vulnerable to the heat, shorten your hike.

Do all of the above and you'll likely experience only joy and fulfillment while hiking in the desert. But if you're able to recognize symptoms of the following ailments, and you know how to treat them, you'll be safer yet:

Heat exhaustion occurs when the body begins producing and/or absorbing more heat than it can dissipate, and when insufficient fluid intake decreases blood flow to vital organs.

initial symptoms
- no thirst • no appetite • little or no urination • cold, clammy skin

advanced symptoms
- profuse sweating • extreme fatigue • headache • loss of coordination • dizziness • fainting • nausea

treatment
- rest • drink • eat

Hot + exhausted = unhappy hiker.

Shade + rest + eat + drink = heat exhaustion averted.

Heatstroke (hyperthermia) is an acute form of heat exhaustion resulting from excessive exposure to extreme heat, prolonged dehydration, and dangerously elevated body temperature.

initial symptoms
• dry skin • high temperature • flushed appearance
• weak, rapid pulse • erratic behavior

advanced symptoms
• headache • nausea • seizures • collapse • shock
• unconsciousness

treatment
• cool the victim immediately: move him to shade, take off his excess clothing, repeatedly douse his head and torso with water, fan him to increase evaporative cooling • seek medical help asap • ideally one person should attend the victim while another initiates a rescue

Water intoxication (hyponatremia) is an abnormally low concentration of sodium in the blood caused by drinking too much water while eating little or nothing.

initial symptoms
• no thirst • no appetite • abnormally frequent, high-volume urination • clear urine

advanced symptoms
• puffy face and fingers • muscle weakness
• erratic behavior • nausea • diarrhea • headache
• unconsciousness

treatment
• rest • eat • swallow small amounts of electrolyte powder instead of mixing it in water • seek medical help asap

Sundown

When the sun sinks in the desert, so does the temperature, perhaps by as much as 40° F (22° C). Rocks and sand don't retain heat. Neither does the dry air. Cloudless nights are especially prone to rapid cooling.

So savvy desert hikers always pack head-to-toe insulation: a fleece hat, fleece gloves, a lightweight shell; a longsleeve, midweight fleece top; and a pair of lightweight fleece tights.

In case it's necessary to hike after sundown, be sure you have a headlamp with fresh batteries. To keep yourself energized, also carry a couple extra Power Bars. Think of them as an essential item in your first-aid kit. You *do* carry a first-aid kit, right?

Legend for Trip Maps		
canyon rim	arch	∩
featured trail	pass	) (
other trail	trailhead	**P**
featured route	highway	
other route	gravel road	
perennial stream	campground	▲
intermittent stream	hiking direction	⟶

East of Corona Arch (Trip 1)

done in a day

the hikes

trip 1

corona arch

location	Potash Road, west of Moab
round trip	3 mi (5 km)
elevation gain	556 ft (170 m)
hiking time	1½ to 2½ hours
difficulty	easy
map	Trails Illustrated *Moab South*

opinion

The most impressive arch in Utah—excluding those enshrined in nearby Arches National Park—is Corona. A testament to its extraordinary size and beauty is that Corona is sometimes called "Little Rainbow Bridge." It does resemble the famous natural bridge on an inlet of Lake Powell, but Corona is unique.

From Moab, the Corona trailhead is closer than that of any arch in the national park. Yet you'll find Corona less crowded, because reaching it requires a 45-minute hike—a fun romp, mostly on slickrock.

Corona is mammoth: 140 ft (43 m) high, 105 ft (32 m) wide. Its setting is equally impressive: on the wall of Bootlegger Canyon, in a huge amphitheater also containing Bowtie Arch.

Bowtie is a bonus sight. It appears that a haywire missile from a passing spacecraft blasted through the back wall of its deep alcove. If so, perhaps one of the alien pilot's many appendages accidentally bumped the ship's controls while all of his eyes were ogling Corona Arch.

Corona Arch

fact

by vehicle

From the junction of Hwys 191 and 128, beside the Colorado River bridge just north of Moab, drive Hwy 191 northwest. Cross the bridge. At 1.6 mi (2.5 km), turn left (southwest) onto Hwy 279 (Potash Road). It soon parallels the river. Continue through the canyon mouth known as *The Portal*. At 11.2 mi (18 km) turn right (east) into the trailhead parking lot. Elevation: 4000 ft (1220 m).

on foot

The trail departs the south end of the parking lot. Switchback upward for a couple minutes, then hike generally northeast. Cross the railroad tracks. Soon curve right (east), then left (northeast).

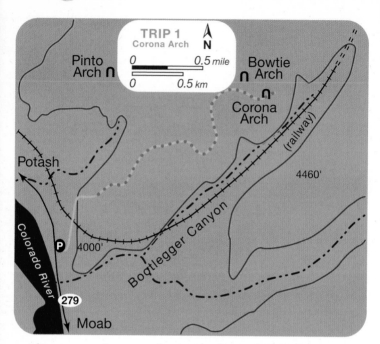

After a very short rough stretch, the trail levels above and the view expands. Look left (north-northeast) for **Pinto Arch** high on the canyon wall. It's right (east) of two deep alcoves. Resume a gradual ascent for about eight minutes, following cairns across slickrock then continuing on the sandy trail.

About 30 minutes from the trailhead, reach 4280 ft (1305 m). After a short descent east to 4200 ft (1280 m), the remainder of the hike is a cairned slickrock route. Reach a fixed, horizontal cable where the terrain steepens.

Around the next corner, **Bowtie Arch** is visible left (north-northeast) in the roof of a deep alcove. But much larger Corona Arch—northeast, at the far end of the amphitheater—is the dominant sight.

Arrive at a vertical cable and a crude-but-effective staircase cut into the sandstone. Then climb a short ladder to complete the ascent onto a slickrock terrace. The way forward is now obvious: simply follow the cairns as you contour through the amphitheater.

You're hiking along the northwest wall of **Bootlegger Canyon**. Gradually curve right (east) along the slickrock terrace. Reach **Corona Arch** at 1.5 mi (2.4 km), 4396 ft (1340 m). Continue beneath and beyond the arch to fully appreciate the impressive setting.

Yes, that's a railroad track you see below. It exits upper Bootlegger Canyon through a tunnel. The train carries potash from the mine down river.

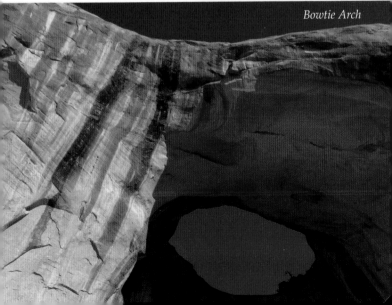

Bowtie Arch

trip 2

morning glory canyon

location	Colorado River Valley, northeast of Moab
round trip	4.6 mi (7.4 km) to Morning Glory
	plus at least 3 mi (4.8 km) exploring
elevation gain	327 ft (100 m) to Morning Glory
	plus at least 246 ft (75 m) exploring
hiking time	2 hours for Morning Glory
	plus at least 2½ hours exploring
difficulty	easy to Morning Glory, moderate beyond
map	Trails Illustrated *Moab South*

opinion

You'll hear the name *Negro Bill* in reference to this canyon and the surrounding Wilderness Study Area. But that's the last you'll hear it from us.

Some names, regardless of historical origin, should be stricken from the record. Otherwise they reinforce attitudes now universally recognized as noxious, repugnant or just plain asinine—in this case all three.

The primary feature distinguishing the canyon is Morning Glory Natural Bridge, the sixth-longest rock span in the U.S. and an arresting sight. So BLM, take note: When you cease your interminable "study" and finally declare this a full-fledged Wilderness Area, change the insensitive name. We propose you officially call it *Morning Glory Canyon*.

Though big—243 ft (74 m) long, to be precise—the namesake bridge is difficult to appreciate until you're directly beneath it. But it's only 2.3 mi (3.7 km) from the trailhead. Besides, the

On the way to
Morning Glory Bridge

Morning Glory Bridge

canyon itself is beautiful, with bulging, soaring, sensuous, Navajo sandstone walls; a clear, perennial stream; lush vegetation including cottonwoods and Gambel oaks; and abundant wildlife ranging from crayfish to hawks.

Plus the going is easy. The short, comfortable trail gains little elevation, so it's ideal for families with hikers-in-training, strong striders seeking a quick-but-scenic workout, or even non-hikers wanting to take a step in the right direction. During spring runoff, you might have to get your feet wet while crossing the stream (bring sandals), but most of the year it's possible to keep your boots dry by rockhopping.

"It's popular" is the worst thing you can say about Morning Glory. The canyon is simply too appealing and close to town to afford solitude. If you're here very early or late in the day, or when the weather's uncomfortably hot or cold, you'll of course see fewer people. But if you're here during prime time along with everyone else, ditch the crowd by out-hiking them.

Almost nobody ventures beyond the natural bridge, yet the canyon extends another eight miles. Our recommendation for experienced navigators, described below, is to briefly head upstream then veer into the intriguing expanse of slickrock above the canyon's north wall. You'll be there in a mere half mile. You can then decide to keep exploring cross-country all the way to overlook the Colorado River Canyon, or imitate the surrounding boulders by stopping, sitting, and silently absorbing the canyon atmosphere.

Follow a perennial stream to Morning Glory Bridge.

Exploring cross-country beyond Morning Glory Canyon

fact

by vehicle

From Hwy 191, at the northwest edge of Moab, turn east onto Hwy 128. Follow it 3 mi (4.8 km), paralleling the Colorado River.

From I-70, near Cisco, drive Hwy 128 generally south, then southwest. Continue 41.5 mi (66.8 km) to milepost 3.

From either approach, turn southeast into the trailhead parking area. Elevation: 4000 ft (1219 m).

on foot

The trail departs the east side of the parking area, right (south) of the map kiosk. Initially lined with rocks, briefly atop slickrock, the trail soon becomes a sandy path heading generally southeast, following the creek upstream, on the left (northeast) bank.

You'll cross the creek several times. Where to do so is always apparent thanks to directional signs, cairns, prominent stepping stones in the water, and the bootprints of previous hikers on the well-worn path.

At 1.3 mi (2.1 km) pass the mouth of a brushy tributary canyon on the right. Proceed on the sandy, main trail. A gentle ascent ensues. After descending back to the creek, cross to the north bank.

About 45 minutes from the trailhead, reach a **junction** at 1.9 mi (3.1 km), 4185 ft (1276 m), near the broad mouth of a second tributary canyon (right / south). The trail left (northeast) continues following the creek up the main canyon. For now, go right (south), cross the creek, and enter the tributary canyon.

The trail ascends steeply about eight minutes to a broad ledge at 4330 ft (1320 m). From here, **Morning Glory Natural Bridge** is visible southeast at the head of the tributary canyon. The optimal view is from directly beneath the bridge, at 2.3 mi (3.7 km), 4327 ft (1319 m).

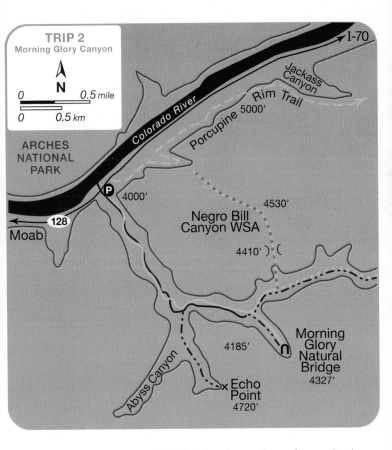

The impressive size of the bridge is not its only merit. As natural bridges go, it's unusual. Most bridges were formed by a stream. That's what distinguishes them from arches, which were created by weathering and/or a combination of erosional forces. But Morning Glory was carved at the base of a waterfall. And the gap separating the bridge from the cliff over which the water cascaded is slim: only 15 ft (4.6 m) wide.

The falls seldom flows these days, but a seep spring near the bridge feeds **Morning Glory pool**. Itch alert: poison ivy is

Exploring slickrock cross-country to Colorado River overlook

prolific here. It has shiny leaves (three per stem), each with serrated edges. Do not touch.

After returning to the tributary mouth, rockhop back to the junction on the creek's north bank. Then either turn left to retrace your steps to the trailhead, or turn right to explore up-canyon (northeast). It's brushy here, so the trail up-canyon might initially be obscure, but it soon becomes obvious again.

In a couple minutes, the trail rises onto a low ledge (left, above the creek), then drops and requires you to briefly tunnel through tamarisk. Soon pass a shallow, steep-walled bay on the left (north) wall of the canyon.

About 10 minutes from the junction, turn left into the second bay on the canyon's north wall. Follow the bootbeaten route. It soon ascends steeply among boulders. About seven minutes from the main canyon floor, reach the **hanging tributary drainage** above, at 4446 ft (1355 m).

Voilà. Flat slickrock at the lip of the drainage invites you to sit, relax, admire the canyon below, and savor the tranquility. But if the intriguing domes farther north tug at your curiosity, keep going. Just be careful to avoid crushing the cryptogamic soil.

In about 15 minutes, you can be atop those domes, gazing at the La Sal Mountains south-southeast. The elevation here is 4530 ft (1381 m). Total hiking distance: 3 mi (4.8 km).

Confident scramblers experienced at cross-country navigation can proceed northwest another 0.75 mi (1.2 km) to overlook the Porcupine Rim trail (popular with mountain bikers) and the Colorado River. If you go, avoid stepping on the profuse cryptogamic soil by hiking on slickrock or in dry watercourses. Continually look back, so you stay oriented and can easily retrace your steps to the trailhead.

Having witnessed the canyon's beauty—ancient history wrought in stone—knowing a little about its recent human history will complete your experience. Here goes...

The canyon's racist name derives from William Granstaff, a prospector and rancher who grazed cattle here during the late 1800s. Nearly a century later, the BLM initiated a study to determine if the canyon qualified for protection as a Wilderness Area. To prevent further damage by ORVs, they built a dirt barrier at the canyon mouth.

This incensed locals who believed the county, not the federal government, owned the canyon. They bulldozed the barrier. When the BLM rebuilt it, the irate, anti-fed, anti-enviro faction again demolished it. Then they spread gravel in the canyon, claimed it was an "improved road" and argued it no longer qualified as "roadless," which is a prerequisite for Wilderness status.

This Sagebrush Rebellion skirmish ended when the federal government filed suit in U.S. district court. The result was a negotiated settlement allowing the Wilderness Area Study to continue, which it supposedly still does.

trip 3
fisher towers

location	Colorado River Valley, northeast of Moab
round trip	4.6 mi (7.4 km)
elevation gain	1050 ft (320 m) including ups & downs
hiking time	2½ to 3½ hours
difficulty	easy
map	Trails Illustrated *Moab North*

opinion

The phantasmagoria of southern Utah inspire imaginative comparisons. "That one looks like…" is the usual response. Which is always interesting. But if these formations were art—as indeed they are, every piece created by the master sculptor Erosion—your admiration wouldn't be limited to free associating. You would ask yourself, "What does it mean? What is it saying?"

The Fisher Towers look like the soaring, ornate, baroque architecture of Belgium, at Brussels' Le Grand Place, or Ghent's Michelmas. Or the ancient, fantastic, erotic shrines at Khajuraho, India, minus the shocking eroticism. But what do the lofty, incomprehensibly intricate Fisher Towers *say*? Perhaps their message is, "Don't endure a mundane existence. Unleash your wild mind. Think original thoughts. Act on them exuberantly. Be an iconoclast and celebrate it."

The trailhead is at the very base of these rippling, filigreed, hardened-mud monoliths. It's surprising how many people shuffle only a few steps from their vehicle, stare open-mouthed, then leave. But the trail winds intimately among the Fisher Towers, affording the hiker a consummately vivid, memorable encounter.

Titan Tower

Despite frequent ups and downs, this short, out-and-back journey is easily galloped in a couple hours. Yet it packs as much scenic wallop as any hike anywhere. Sweeping vistas across the Colorado River Valley and into the La Sal Mountains complement the reach-out-and-touch-'em views of the towers. Upon your arrival in the Moab area, even if it's late afternoon, come here to stretch your legs, jettison humdrum concerns, and disengage your duty-burdened brain.

Tallest of the towers, the 900-ft (274-m) Titan, was first summitted in 1962 by three Coloradoans. Climbing sandstone was dicey as space travel then but is less so now thanks to improved hardware. Climbers achieve an even greater affinity with the Fisher Towers than do hikers. It's the difference between peering into a kaleidoscope and being in one.

fact

by vehicle

From Hwy 191, at the northwest edge of Moab, turn east onto Hwy 128. Follow it 21 mi (33.8 km), paralleling the Colorado River. At milepost 21, turn right (east-southeast) onto unpaved Fisher Road, signed *Fisher Towers*.

From I-70, near Cisco, drive Hwy 128 generally south 23.5 mi (37.8 km). Turn left (east-southeast) onto unpaved Fisher Road, signed *Fisher Towers*.

From either approach, proceed 2.2 mi (3.5 km) to the trailhead parking area near the base of the towers. Elevation: 4720 ft (1440 m).

There's a small BLM campground here. It has pit toilets, tables, and fire grills, but no water. The chimney-like pinnacle of Castle Rock is visible south-southwest. Beyond it is Porcupine Rim.

on foot

The trail departs the south-southwest corner of the parking area, between the metal register and the wood sign. Immediately

Fisher Towers

descend a short staircase, curve left, then begin a gradual ascent generally south. Initially the trail is lined with rocks. In about six minutes, follow a sign directing you left, through a **cleft**, down into a wash.

In about 30 minutes, reach a level **shoulder** affording a sweeping view of intricate tower walls and odd sandstone formations. From here, the trail curves left (northeast) then gently ascends around another shallow gully. At 1 mi (1.6 km) reach the base of the 900-ft (274-m) **Titan**, tallest of the towers.

About 45 minutes from the trailhead, a 4-rung metal ladder helps you drop into a gully. Ascend the other side via short, accommodating ledges. Ten minutes farther, leave the tower alleyways and ascend to a level **saddle** on a peninsula, at 2.2 mi (3.5 km), 5430 ft (1655 m). It's possible to continue in two directions: briefly right, or much farther left.

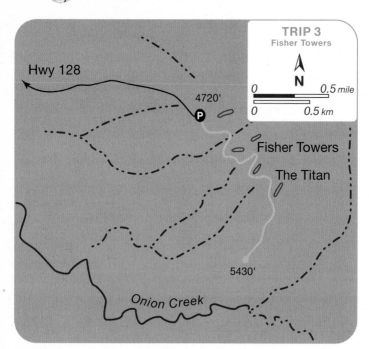

Right (south-southwest) from the saddle, the **main trail ends** within four minutes (mostly level) at an **overlook** above Onion Creek canyon. The distant view north-northwest is upstream into the Colorado River Valley. You've now hiked about an hour from the trailhead.

To proceed left (east) from the saddle, look right for bootprints revealing a short, narrow trough—the easiest way to step down. Then contour left (east), following more bootprints. Ascend between boulders.

About four minutes from the saddle, reach a fairly level **expanse of slickrock** affording a view north to the back of the towers and overlooking a startlingly deep southward drainage. From here it's possible to ramble 15 minutes or so farther—up and down the convoluted slickrock ridge—generally south. The edges are precipitous, but it's safe if you find the correct passage.

From the expanse of slickrock, turn your back to the towers and head south. Look right for a **small natural bridge**. Scramble beneath it to continue. Bear left (east). Bootprints in the sand will probably guide you.

Ascend over a promontory. On its left (east) side, skirt the edge of the 1000-ft (305-m) abyss. Be sure footed. Figure your way toward the final, **bulbous sandstone formation** where a sheer cliff halts progress. Onion Creek is visible below. Fisher Valley Ranch is southeast, backed by Manti La Sal National Forest.

Prickly pear cacti

trip 4

professor creek / mary jane canyon

location	Colorado River Valley, northeast of Moab
round trip	8.7 mi (14 km)
elevation gain	410 ft (125 m)
hiking time	4 to 5 hours
difficulty	easy
map	Trails Illustrated *Moab North*

opinion

Think of Moab as an acronym for *Moments Of Absolute Bliss*. Not the town itself, but the surrounding area, where a profusion of sublime trails keeps hikers elated. One of them is a short, easy jaunt, following Professor Creek into Mary Jane Canyon.

Less than an hour from the trailhead, you'll find yourself in a narrowing, deepening, sinuous, red-rock ravine. The walls amplify the creek's delicate water music, bathing you in omniphonic sound. You've entered a tiny wrinkle in the earth's skin and discovered a beautiful, soothing sanctuary.

If canyon-fired curiosity quickens your pace, another hour will bring you to where Mary Jane Canyon pinches shut, denying further exploration to all but commando canyoneers. Here, a dual-spouted waterfall gushes over a huge chokestone shaped like a snake's head. Time to stop, contemplate, absorb.

Succumb to mesmerism and you'll see the rock reptile's head is cocked to one side. His eyes are closed. His smile is that of

Mary Jane Canyon

Heading southeast up Professor Creek, toward Adobe Mesa

a benevolent Buddha. He's a beatific beast, luxuriating in this cool, peaceful refuge, inviting you to commune with him.

By southern Utah standards, Mary Jane is a modest canyon. And Professor Creek, except during a rare, brief freshet, is a tame, meandering trickle. The water depth varies seasonally, according to how much snow is melting in Manti-La Sal National Forest and how much rain has recently fallen. It's usually ankle- to calf-deep. Despite their humble dimensions, however, the creek and canyon tantalize and ultimately enthrall.

The creek's generally low flow gives you a choice: wear sandals, slosh through, get wet; or wear boots and stay dry by rockhopping frequently with the aid of trekking poles. Base your decision on the air and water temperatures. On a hot day in desert canyon country, walking in water is exhilarating yet soothing. Do it if possible. Opportunities like this are rare. Another water-walk near Moab is Mill Creek Canyon (page 26).

fact

by vehicle

From Hwy 191, at the northwest edge of Moab, turn east onto Hwy 128. Follow it 18.4 mi (29.6 km), paralleling the Colorado River. Just before milepost 19 and the sign *Onion Creek 2*, turn right (east-southeast) onto a well-graded dirt road.

From I-70, near Cisco, drive Hwy 128 generally south 26.1 mi (42 km). Turn left (east-southeast) onto a dirt road signed *Ranch Road, Dead End.*

Professor Creek cascade where a chokestone halts hikers' progress in upper Mary Jane Canyon

From either approach, reset your trip odometer to 0 and proceed on the ranch road. At 1.6 mi (2.6 km), bear right (east-southeast). At 1.7 mi (2.7 km), continue straight where a road forks right. Curve right at 1.9 mi (3 km), passing a homesite on the left. At 2.1 mi (3.4 km) pass a fenced diversion dam on the right. At 3.5 mi (2.2 km), where the road bends right (southwest) toward Castle Rock and the Priest & Nuns formation visible on the horizon, park in a clearing on the left. Elevation: 4335 ft (1322 m).

on foot

From the parking area, drop to **Professor Creek**. Cross it, bear right, and hike upstream (southeast) along the bank. Southeast will remain your general direction of travel until trail's end.

Soon cross back to the right (south) bank. Cottonwood and juniper trees grace the initially very shallow drainage. The creek originates as creeklets draining Fisher Mesa (left / east) and Adobe Mesa (right / south-southeast).

If it's hot, and you're wearing sandals or footwear you don't mind soaking, then splash through the water. (Before plunging in, judge the water temperature. It can be frigid in

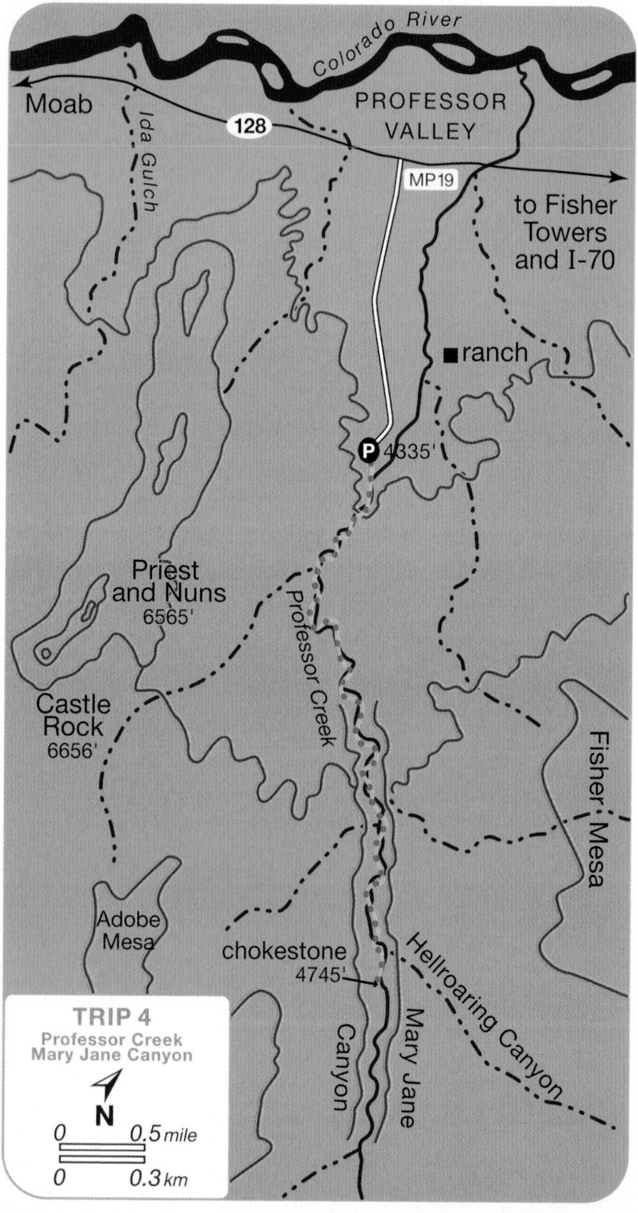

Colorado River

Moab

PROFESSOR VALLEY

128

MP 19

to Fisher Towers and I-70

Ida Gulch

■ ranch

P 4335'

Priest and Nuns 6565'

Professor Creek

Castle Rock 6656'

Fisher Mesa

Adobe Mesa

chokestone 4745'

Hellroaring Canyon

Mary Jane Canyon

Canyon

TRIP 4
Professor Creek
Mary Jane Canyon

N

0   0.5 mile

0   0.3 km

spring and fall.) Otherwise, depending on the creek's depth, it's possible to keep your boots dry, but you'll have to cross and re-cross frequently to attain whichever bank affords easier hiking. Most of the way, a bootbeaten path is evident, suggesting where to switch to the opposite bank, or where to leave the creekbed and shortcut sandy benches.

About 30 minutes from the trailhead, the drainage walls are noticeably higher. You're entering **Mary Jane Canyon**. At this point, it's about 80 ft (24 m) wide and 65 ft (20 m) deep. Continue following the creek upstream, passing several side canyons—usually dry.

At about 2.3 mi (3.7 km), 4565 ft (1392 m), a little more than one hour from the trailhead, the canyon is 130 ft (40 m) to 180 ft (55 m) deep. Proceed through **narrows** for the next 2 mi (3.2 km).

A double-tongued **waterfall** flowing over a chokestone at 4.3 mi (6.9 km), 4745 ft (1447 m), halts upstream progress for most of us. Fast hikers will arrive here within two hours.

Colorado River canyon, from Highway 128

trip 5

big spring canyon/ squaw canyon

location	Canyonlands National Park, Needles District
loop	7.5 mi (12.1 km)
elevation gain	430 ft (131 m)
hiking time	3 to 3½ hours
difficulty	easy
map	Trails Illustrated *Canyonlands National Park / Needles & Island in the Sky*

opinion

Problems ooze from every facet of life, often squirting into our faces when least expected. Why are solutions so scarce and reclusive, skulking in crevices until yanked out by their ears? At least this hike is an exception: a brilliant solution generously presents itself precisely when needed.

You'll hike up Big Spring Canyon, down Squaw Canyon. It's a short, easy, tantalizing preview of the loop and circuit dayhiking available on the 60-mi (96.6-km) trail network in Canyonlands' Needles District. These two particular canyons are separated in their upper reaches by an imposing slickrock wall. To hikers nearing the wall, it looks insurmountable. Proceed. The way will appear. But not until you're upon it. So the approach is an intriguing mystery. And the climax—a welcoming passageway amid steep, complex slickrock—feels like a gift.

Before and after breaching this concealed crux, you'll walk through beautiful high-desert environs: piñon and juniper

Desert varnish on walls of Big Spring Canyon

forest, sandy washes, mushroom buttes, slickrock ridges, red-rock canyons. Only the culminating, 400-ft (122-m) high wall, however, is striking. Elsewhere along this trail, the immediate topography averages a mere 100 ft (30 m) high—impressive if you're new to canyon country, piddling compared to the soaring sides of Paria Canyon near Kanab, Spring Canyon in Capitol Reef Park, and many others.

Warning: The route linking Big Spring and Squaw canyons is briefly precipitous—ascending and descending. It might make acrophobes anxious.

Encouragement: Even if it's afternoon when you arrive in the Needles District, scamper around this loop. It will lend a sense of accomplishment to your day. The final 1.1 mi (1.8 km) is straightforward, easy to follow at dusk.

October storm, Big Spring Canyon

fact

before your trip

If you intend to dayhike in the area for a few days, try to camp at Squaw Flat. The campground has water (spring through fall) and toilets. The 26 sites, each with picnic table and fire pit, are available first come, first served. If the campground's full—which it usually is during peak season—arrive by 10 a.m., watch for someone to leave, then claim their vacated site.

by vehicle

From Moab, drive Hwy 191 south 38.5 mi (62 km). Or, from Monticello, drive Hwy 191 north 13.5 mi (21.7 km). From either approach, turn west onto Hwy 211, signed *Canyonlands National Park, Needles District.* (A few miles north of this junction is a road west signed *Needles Overlook*, which is *not* your destination.)

Heading west on Hwy 211, pass Newspaper Rock—a must see—at 12.3 mi (19.8 km). Reach the Visitor Center at 35 mi (56.4 km). Continue another 2.5 mi (4 km) generally southwest following signs for Squaw Flat Campground. Turn left to enter campground loop A. The paved trailhead parking area is just ahead. Shortly before the road ends, park on the left, near the toilets. Elevation: 5180 ft (1580 m).

on foot

A sandy path departs the trailhead, near the toilets. Follow it south. Reach a **fork** within two minutes. Left (southeast) leads to Squaw Canyon and the Peekaboo trail (Trip 8). You'll return that way. For now, go right (southwest) toward Big Spring Canyon.

The trail soon crosses a small slickrock **ridge**. The Needles are visible west-southwest. About 10 minutes from the trailhead, reach another **junction**. Right (north) returns to Squaw Flat Campground loop B. Go left (southwest) for Big Spring Canyon.

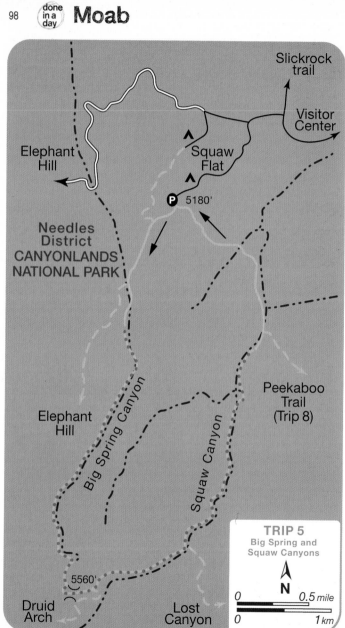

Slickrock trail

Visitor Center

Elephant Hill

Squaw Flat

P 5180'

Needles District
CANYONLANDS
NATIONAL PARK

Elephant Hill

Big Spring Canyon

Squaw Canyon

Peekaboo Trail
(Trip 8)

5560'

Druid Arch

Lost Canyon

TRIP 5
Big Spring and
Squaw Canyons

N

0   0.5 mile
0   1 km

At 1.2 mi (1.6 km), having hiked about 20 minutes, arrive at an important **junction** in Big Spring Canyon. Right (southwest) leads to Chesler Park in 3.7 mi (6 km) and Druid Arch in 6.2 mi (10 km). Go left (south) to proceed into Big Spring Canyon and loop back to Squaw Flat Campground in 6.3 mi (3.8 km). Left also leads to Druid Arch in 7.2 mi (11.6 km). So the Druid circuit returns to this junction; see Trip 10d for details.

Scarlet gilia in April

Proceeding left (south) into **Big Spring Canyon**, pass backcountry **campsite** BS2 at 5180 ft (1580 m), about 40 minutes from the trailhead. Shortly beyond, the sandy trail goes left and launches onto a cairned slickrock bench. Gain 60 ft (18 m) in the next 10 minutes, cross the **creekbed**, then ascend left (southeast) following cairns.

Head south through a 20-ft (6-m) wide **wash** full of rock slabs. Soon, at a huge **wall**, the route rises onto a bench and becomes fascinating. Swift hikers will be here in 1¼ hours.

Climb slickrock steps beneath huge mushroom-shaped rocks to your left. Follow cairns over the slickrock saddle. Left of the huge wall, a **passageway**—concealed from below—is now apparent. Top out at 5560 ft (1695 m) and savor the view before dropping southeast. Below (northeast) is Squaw Canyon. Distant west-northwest are two singular pinnacles: North and South Six-shooter peaks. Chesler Park is west. North-northwest is Island in the Sky—the evocatively named mesa dominating the north half of Canyonlands Park (Trips 7 and 9).

From the saddle, descend 140 ft (42 m) on slickrock. Reach a signed **junction** on the edge of the slickrock, at 3.8 mi (6.1 km). Right (east-southeast) along the slickrock ridge leads 2.1 mi (3.4 km) to Elephant Canyon—potential access to Druid Arch and Chesler Park. Go left (northeast) along the slickrock ridge in the opposite direction, heading for Squaw Flat Campground, 3.7 mi (6 km) distant.

About 20 minutes from the saddle, reach a **junction** at 4.7 mi (7.6 km), 5220 ft (1590 m). Right (south) leads 5.7 mi (9.2 km) to Peekaboo Camp, via Lost Canyon. Go left (east) in **Squaw Canyon**. It has 100-ft (30-m) walls and a sandy floor shaded by cottonwood and oak trees.

The trail briefly crosses a grassy "park" before reaching a **junction** at 6.4 mi (10.3 km). Right (southeast) is the Peekaboo trail (Trip 8), an extraordinary slickwalk. Go left (northwest). Soon traverse two, small slickrock **bluffs** separated by sand. After descending the second bluff, a level, sandy path leads 300 yd (330 m) to Squaw Flat Campground and the completion of your 7.5-mi (12.1-km) loop.

Evening primrose

Primrose blooming during a wet October

trip 6

devils garden

location	Arches National Park
loop	7.7 mi (12.4 km) including all digressions
elevation gain	650 ft (198 m)
hiking time	3½ to 4 hours
difficulty	easy
map	Trails Illustrated *Arches National Park*

opinion

Devils Garden, in Arches National Park, harbors the highest concentration of significant natural arches on earth. Among them is Landscape Arch—an impossibly slender ribbon of stone longer than a football field. It ranks among our planet's greatest natural wonders.

For notoriety, Landscape Arch competes with nearby Delicate Arch (see front cover and page 21). Both are composed of Entrada sandstone. But because Landscape Arch is horizontal, it's not as photogenic as Delicate Arch, whose compact, vertical profile fits stylishly on Utah postage stamps and license plates and has thus become emblematic of the American southwest.

Landscape is the world's longest natural arch. It's a smidge longer than the runner-up, Kolob Arch in Zion National Park. Landscape is also incomparably elegant, which is why most observers consider it a more astounding sight than Kolob. It's certainly easier to reach. Viewing Kolob necessitates a 14-mi (22.5-km) round-trip dayhike. Landscape is a mere one mile from the trailhead.

And what a trailhead it is: 150 paved parking stalls, all of which are frequently occupied because this is the most popular

Freelancing in Devils Garden

trail in the park. "Trail," however, is initially a euphemism. A broad, smooth, pedestrian highway leads to Landscape Arch. Beyond, it diminishes to an actual trail, then tapers to what the park calls a "primitive" trail. So most visitors—unfit, unambitious, unprepared for a genuine hike, and incurious—turn around after ogling Landscape, allowing you to continue in relative tranquility.

The crowd always misses the finer points, of course. What they miss here is the longest maintained trail in the park—a loop revealing numerous arches less miraculous than Landscape but equally beautiful and enthralling. Because these arches are sequestered, they tend to be in unexpected, intimate settings, so you're apt to feel an exhilarating sense of discovery when you finally clap eyes on them. With luck (boost yours by hiking very early or late in the day), solitude will enrich your experience.

The Devils Garden hike reveals but a fraction of the national park's more than 2,000 catalogued arches. They range in size from a three-foot opening—the minimum to be considered an arch—to the implausible, taffy-pull expanse of Landscape Arch. Though all are solid stone, and many appear stalwart, they're impermanent, even fragile. Created by 100 million years of erosion (wind, water, ice) and weathering (decomposition), they will eventually succumb to the same forces that created them and the inexorable pull of gravity. Likewise, new arches are slowly being created. So the art here is constantly changing, just as it does in any gallery.

While admiring the more horizontal arches, particularly Landscape Arch, you might wonder: "Is it really an arch? Or is it actually a bridge?" Though somewhat arbitrary, there *is* a distinction—enough to justify the name *Natural Bridges National Monument* for another of Utah's scenic treasure troves, farther south. An arch is formed by weathering and/or a combination of erosional forces. A natural bridge is a type of natural arch, but one primarily formed by flowing water.

Landscape Arch

fact

before your trip

If you're intent on photographing Landscape Arch in optimal light, begin hiking early in the morning, when the sun will illuminate the arch from behind you.

by vehicle

From the junction of Hwys 191 and 128, beside the Colorado River bridge just north of Moab, drive Hwy 191 northwest. Cross the bridge. At 2 mi (3.2 km) turn right (north) to enter Arches National Park. From the visitor center, stay on the main park road another 17.2 mi (27.8 km) to its north terminus at the Devil's Garden trailhead parking lot. Elevation: 5180 ft (1579 m).

on foot

Follow the road-width, gravel trail northwest through slickrock fins. Within five minutes begin a moderate ascent on steps.

These fins formed when the earth rose beneath a solid layer of sandstone, which fractured into long, parallel, vertical ridges that allowed the arches to develop.

At 0.3 mi (0.5 km) a right spur affords a 0.6-mi (1-km) round-trip digression to **Pinetree and Tunnel arches**. Both are relatively young, in other words small, but they're a fitting prelude to the exceedingly old arch you'll see next.

Resuming northwest on the main trail, reach a fork at 0.9 mi (1.4 km), 5230 ft (1594 m). Right, heading generally north-northwest, is the so-called Primitive trail. You'll return that way if you follow our suggested loop, so for now proceed left (northwest).

Landscape Arch is visible left (west) at 1 mi (1.6 km). Roughly 306 ft (93 m) long and 105 ft (32 m) high, it narrows to an astonishingly scant 11 ft (3.4 m). Judging by the first known photo of Landscape Arch, taken in 1896, it has changed very little during the intervening years. Nevertheless, it could collapse at any time. Since 1991, portions of the arch have broken off and fallen to the ground, which is why walking beneath it is now prohibited.

Continuing northwest on the main trail, briefly follow cairns across slickrock while ascending between fins. Soon pass **Wall Arch** (right / northeast). Beyond, begin climbing moderately to steeply on sand and slickrock.

At 1.3 mi (2.1 km), 5450 ft (1661 m), a left (southwest) spur affords a 0.7-mi (1.1-km) round-trip digression to **Navajo Arch and Partition Arch**. Both are compelling sights in secretive locations. Navajo, rooted in smooth gravel, is graceful despite its hefty girth. Partition comprises two, nearly round arches—separated by a stone "partition"—in one wall.

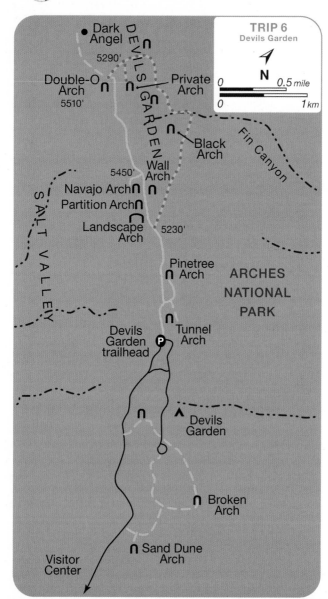

TRIP 6
Devils Garden

N

0   0.5 mile
0   1 km

Dark Angel •
DEVILS GARDEN
5290'
Double-O Arch
5510'
Private Arch
Black Arch
Fin Canyon
Wall Arch
5450'
Navajo Arch
Partition Arch
Landscape Arch
5230'
SALT VALLEY
Pinetree Arch
ARCHES NATIONAL PARK
Tunnel Arch
Devils Garden trailhead P
Devils Garden
Broken Arch
Visitor Center
Sand Dune Arch

Back on the main trail, resume hiking west-northwest. Soon enjoy expansive views. Walk over slickrock and atop fins to reach the next junction at 2.2 mi (3.5 km), 5510 ft (1679 m)—the loop highpoint. Right (north) quickly ends at a viewpoint overlooking **Black Arch** in Fin Canyon. Go left (west) for Double-O Arch. See photo, inside front cover.

A few minutes farther, **Double-O Arch** is visible left. Proceed to the foot of the arch by descending northwest atop a slickrock fin then curving west among large piñon pines. Double-O comprises a big arch directly above a smaller one. To appreciate it fully, proceed through the lower arch to the southwest side and ascend slightly.

Immediately below and beyond Double-O is a junction at 2.3 mi (3.7 km). Left (west) is a spur affording a 1-mi (1.6-km) round-trip digression to a desert-varnished spire called **Dark Angel**—a solitary remnant of an ancient fin. The views en route are vast, but the spire itself is underwhelming. Go right (north-northwest) to loop back to the trailhead via the **Primitive trail**.

The name "Primitive" and a sign warning of "difficult hiking" ahead are intended to discourage neophytes. Experienced, intermediate hikers who are reasonably cautious and keep to this smaller yet distinct trail will face no obstacles of note—*if* the slickrock is not icy.

The Primitive trail gently descends into a dry wash and curves northeast between fins. Reach a junction at 2.7 mi (4.3 km), 5290 ft (1612 m). The right (southeast) spur affords a 0.4-mi (0.6-km) round-trip digression to **Private Arch**. Hidden among nearby fins, this massive-yet-sensuous arch is an engaging spectacle. (See inside back cover.)

Continuing the loop, the main trail itself soon commands attention and keeps you entertained as it descends via slickrock ramps and ledges, past magnificent piñon trees, to the sandy floor of **Fin Canyon** at 5100 ft (1554 m)—the loop lowpoint.

The Primitive trail maneuvers through this squadron of sandstone fins.

Be alert. At the sign *Trail Leaves Wash*, turn right and begin a brief ascent out of the canyon. The trail levels again, heading generally south-southeast. The La Sal Mountains are visible left (southeast).

Reach a T-junction at 4.4 mi (7.1 km), 5230 ft (1594 m). You're now on familiar ground. Right (northwest) leads 0.1 mi (0.2 km) to Landscape Arch. Turn left and hike southeast 0.9 mi (1.4 km) back to the trailhead parking lot.

trip 7

⟨A⟩ murphy hogback

location	Canyonlands National Park, Island in the Sky District
circuit	9.75 mi (15.7 km)
elevation gain	1240 ft (378 m)
hiking time	4 to 5 hours
difficulty	moderate
map	Trails Illustrated *Canyonlands National Park / Needles & Island in the Sky*

opinion

From airy vantages in southern Utah, gazing across canyon country is like staring up at a clear night sky. The baffling, dizzying, overwhelming complexity of the earth's surface is as unfathomable as an infinite, star-filled universe. The Island in the Sky District of Canyonlands affords many such spectacles. And the Murphy Hogback trail invites you to leap into one.

It's not an easy invitation to accept. After quickly spurting from trailhead to canyon edge, the trail performs a swooping 1240-ft (378-m) dive onto the White Rim. "Whoa. Why give up this view to trudge all the way down there and back?" you wonder. Well, for the same reason you don't just stare at an artfully presented gourmet meal. You devour it. Hard to believe now, but only after the hike will you fully appreciate the view. Because only then will it be enriched with understanding and accomplishment.

Specific reasons to take the plunge: Astounding passages are thrilling to hike, and this is certainly one. Yet it's not dangerous, despite how unnerving it might be to watch your companions negotiate the skinny ledges. You'll marvel at the daring or

The Murphy trail descends off Island in the Sky.

desperate Murphy brothers who in 1918 contrived this unlikely cattle route down sheer cliffs of Wingate sandstone, and crumbling, sliding, Chinle formation talus slopes. (Imagine their pathetic beasts, bug-eyed with fright.)

There are vistas down there you can't see, or even imagine, from above. Hiking the hogback—a narrow ridge with a level top—you'll marvel at distant views left and right. If you've ever considered mountainbiking the famous White Rim Loop, here's your chance to grok it in a single day, on foot.

Granted, the wash you'll follow en route to the White Rim Road gradually loses its intrigue, but the rest of the journey more than compensates. Even the wash is rewarding to observant hikers who notice the colorful blend of stones underfoot, admire the artful erosion patterns of the maroon and lavender Moenkopi formation, and remember to glance back at the looming Island in the Sky.

Oh yeah, and what about that dreaded return ascent? Quit worrying. Hardened hikers do it in 25 minutes or less.

A couple reminders before you go. Shade is nil, so save this trip for a cool day. You'll find no water en route, so pack more than you think you'll need, and leave a full bottle in your vehicle for when you return.

fact

before your trip

Two trails depart this trailhead. One is very short: just 2 mi (3.2 km) to Murphy Point. But beyond 1 mi (1.6 km) you can camp there, if you get a permit from the Visitor Center. Murphy Point affords a spectacular view, so this is an appealing option before or after your Murphy Hogback hike.

by vehicle

From the junction of Hwys 191 and 128, at the northwest edge of Moab, drive Hwy 191 northwest 8.5 mi (13.7 km) and turn left.

From I-70, drive Hwy 191 southeast 20.3 mi (32.7 km) and turn right. From either approach, reset your trip odometer and drive southwest on Hwy 313 signed *Canyonlands, Island in the Sky*.

At 14.5 mi (23.4 km), pass the road to Dead Horse Point State Park (left / east). Shortly beyond, Navajo Mtn and the Henry Mountains are visible on the horizon (right / west).

At 19.2 mi (30.9 km) enter Canyonlands National Park. At 21.6 mi (34.8 km) arrive at the Visitor Center. At the 27.7-mi (44.6-km) junction, go left for Murphy Point.

At 30.1 mi (48.5 km) turn right (west) into the unpaved parking area. Previously, it was possible to continue driving 0.5 mi (0.8 km), but severe erosion now prevents this. Walk that distance ten minutes to reach the trailhead at road's end. Elevation: 6120 ft (1866 m). Our trail distances do not include this additional 1 mi (1.6 km) round trip.

on foot

The old road right (northwest) is blocked by logs, effectively converting it to trail. Mostly level, it leads 1.3 mi (2.1 km) to **Murphy Point**—a magnificent overlook offering a variation on the Murphy Hogback scenery, but not an improvement.

So, from the end of the former road, fork left (south-southwest) onto the trail signed *White Rim 4.3 miles*. Following our directions, you'll reach the White Rim via the wash and return via the hogback.

Initially, the trail is a level, narrow, sandy trough beelining through piñon and juniper forest. Brief slickrock sections are cairned. Within 15 minutes approach the **canyon rim** at 0.75 mi (1.2 km). Logs placed by rangers funnel you to where the trail begins descending left (east) through a break in the rim.

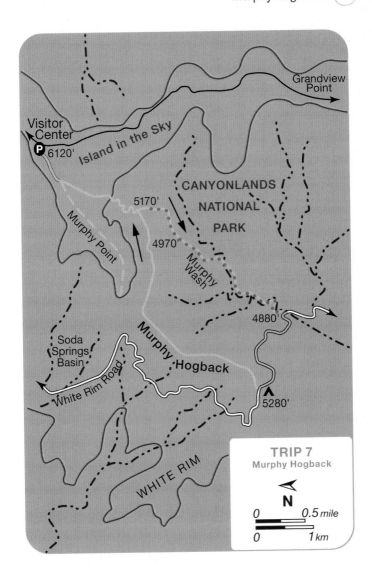

Grandview Point

Visitor Center

P 6120'

Island in the Sky

CANYONLANDS NATIONAL PARK

5170'

Murphy Point

4970'

Murphy Wash

4880'

Soda Springs Basin

Murphy Hogback

White Rim Road

5280'

WHITE RIM

TRIP 7
Murphy Hogback

N

0   0.5 mile

0   1 km

The catwalk allowing hikers to descend the Murphy trail

Ledges on the upper canyon wall afford a surprisingly gentle, switchbacking descent. About five minutes down, reach a **talus slope** of broken rock and boulders. Tight zigzags ensue. Then longer switchbacks resume. A sturdy, **wood** bridge enables the trail to traverse a sheer rock face.

At 1.25 mi (2 km), 5170 ft (1576 m), reach a **signed junction** near the bottom of the talus. From the trailhead, you've now hiked about 45 minutes and descended 950 ft (290 m). Surrounded by boulders and junipers, this is a secluded, peaceful setting where you can gaze up at the rim and out at deepening canyons beyond.

The trail forks here. Right (south-southwest) runs out along Murphy Hogback. Left (south-southeast) descends to the White Rim Road via the wash. The two trails meet at Murphy Camp. Go either way. If you turn left, following our directions, you'll hike the loop clockwise and appreciate Murphy Point's dramatic, red cliffs on the return.

Turning left (south-southeast) at the junction, begin a gentle descent into the **wash**. Soon leave trees behind. Within 15 minutes, the wash is about 6 yd / m deep. Boulders diminish as it broadens. The bottom becomes sandy and level. Notice where overhangs have collapsed due to deep undercutting of the banks: obviously an imprudent place for a shady rest. Pass a cow pen—crudely made, long-ago abandoned. The elevation here is 4970 ft (1515 m).

White Rim Road, Canyonlands National Park

Overlooking Canyonlands from the Murphy trail

Reach the **White Rim Road** at 3.75 mi (6 km), 4880 ft (1488 m). Turn right and follow it uphill, curving west-northwest. About 25 minutes farther, at 5030 ft (1534 m), near a sharp boulder on the right, the road begins climbing steeply.

Surmount **Murphy Hogback** at 5.25 mi (8.5 km), 5280 ft (1610 m). Immediately ahead is **Murphy Camp A**, with a panoramic view. It has tent sites and a pit toilet, but no water and no trash cans. Pack out everything you packed in.

From Camp A, proceed generally north on the road a couple minutes farther. After passing Camp B, but before the road swings left (west), look for a **trail forking right** (northeast). It's signed *Murphy Trailhead 4.5 mi (7.2 km)*. Depart the road and follow this sandy path through scrub. It will soon be apparent you're hiking atop a narrow ridge—the Murphy Hogback.

About five minutes from the road, veer left (northwest), off trail, to the edge of the hogback and a commanding **vista**.

About 425 ft (130 m) below is the White Rim Road. You can see it plunge off the hogback, then wiggle north into Soda Springs Basin. A short stretch of the Green River is visible west/northwest, where it enters Stillwater Canyon after wrapping around a butte called Turks Head (northwest).

Reach the **base of Murphy Point** about 30 minutes after leaving Murphy Camp. Here, at 5200 ft (1585 m), cairns indicate where the trail curves right (east) to exit the hogback and skirt the **red cliffs**.

About 25 minutes farther, having hiked a total of 8.5 mi (13.7 km), arrive at the **signed junction** you previously encountered upon descending from the rim. You've now completed the loop and are on terra cognita. All that remains is the ascent.

Fast hikers regain the rim in 25 minutes. The view is still astounding, yet now intimately familiar. To conclude the 9.75-mi (15.7-km) circuit, stride 15 minutes through piñon and juniper forest to the **trailhead**.

Daisies

trip 8
⊗ peekaboo

location	Canyonlands National Park, Needles District
round trip	10 mi (16.2 km)
elevation gain	940 ft (287 m)
hiking time	6 to 7 hours
difficulty	moderate
map	Trails Illustrated *Canyonlands National Park / Needles & Island in the Sky*

opinion

Many other canyon-country hikes are longer, wilder, lonelier, more challenging, more scenic. But the Peekaboo trail gets straight A's: amusing, amazing, awakening. It's the pièce de résistance of slickwalks. Think roller coaster, on foot. It ramps up, runs along ridges, nips over saddles, wraps around fins, hops onto bluffs, contours through drainages, slides into chutes, fakes left, veers right, even pops through a tiny window to earn its name. About the only thing it doesn't do is lose you along the way.

Fantastically tortuous terrain like this is common in southern Utah canyon country. But much of it would bamfoozle even a champion orienteer. What distinguishes the Peekaboo trail is that it's clearly indicated on maps and precisely cairned by national park rangers, allowing the average hiker to confidently follow its sinuous course. And unlike many slickrock areas near Moab, only hikers are allowed on Peekaboo. No mountain bikes. No motorcycles. No jeeps.

Following the Peekaboo trail across slickrock.
Six-shooter Peak, distant right.

Although the national park refers to it as a trail, most of it is actually a route with nothing but the occasional cairn to indicate the way. You can follow a trail mindlessly. A route, especially a slickrock route, and this one in particular, requires you to be fully engaged. Often, the way forward is a mystery until your boots are upon it. Twice, there wouldn't *be* a way forward if not for strategically placed ladders. This is land you must grapple with mentally and emotionally, as well as physically. That's why Peekaboo is an extraordinarily fulfilling hike.

Rejuvenating is another way to describe it. Parents are forever going on about the pleasure of seeing life through their children's eyes. Well, hiking can top that easily. It can *make* you a kid again. Surprise, discovery, wonder and delight are impossible to suppress while giddily romping the Peekaboo. Ultimately, the experience transcends even the innocence of childhood, offering a sense of grace, of sanctification.

Which begs a question. Was it really just the mechanical processes of geology that aimlessly wrinkled this land? Or was there intent? The intent to inspire play and elicit joy among all creatures who wander here?

fact

before your trip

If you intend to dayhike in the area for a few days, try to camp at Squaw Flat. The campground has water (spring through fall) and toilets. The 26 sites, each with picnic table and fire pit, are available first come, first served. If the campground's full—which it usually is during peak season—arrive by 10 a.m., watch for someone to leave, then claim their vacated site.

by vehicle

From Moab, drive Hwy 191 south 38.5 mi (62 km). Or, from Monticello, drive Hwy 191 north 13.5 mi (21.7 km). From either approach, turn west onto Hwy 211, signed *Canyonlands National Park, Needles District*. (A few miles north of this junction is a road west signed *Needles Overlook*, which is *not* your destination.)

Heading west on Hwy 211, pass Newspaper Rock—a must see—at 12.3 mi (19.8 km). Reach the Visitor Center at 35 mi (56.4 km). Continue another 2.5 mi (4 km) generally southwest following signs for Squaw Flat Campground. Turn left to enter campground loop A. The paved trailhead parking area is just ahead. Shortly before the road ends, park on the left, near the toilets. Elevation: 5180 ft (1580 m).

on foot

A sandy path departs the trailhead, near the toilets. Follow it south. Reach a **fork** within two minutes. Right (southwest) leads to Big Spring Canyon (Trip 5) and Druid Arch (Trip 10d). Go left (southeast) toward Squaw Canyon.

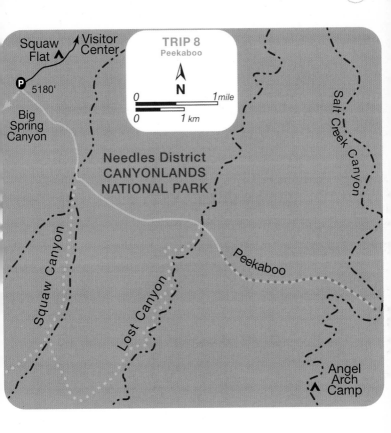

In 330 yd (300 m) ascend over a small slickrock **bluff**. After a sandy stretch, traverse another, similar **bluff**. About 20 minutes from the trailhead, reach a **junction** at 1.1 mi (1.8 km). Right (south) probes Squaw Canyon (Trip 5). Go left (southeast) on the Peekaboo trail, soon among gambel oaks.

About 40 minutes from the trailhead, ascend slickrock to 5240 ft (1598 m). Then drop 12 yd/m and curve left (east) following cairns. Descend from red slickrock to white, to yellow, to black. Curve right (south) to where a metal **ladder** grants passage over a ledge.

Salt Creek Canyon

Even with the ladder, the descent requires awareness. From there, go left (south-southeast) on white-and-tan slickrock. The route then drops into a sandy **wash** and becomes a trail among cottonwoods, juniper and piñon.

Heading southeast, the trail rises out of the wash onto sage flats. Reach a **junction** at 2.6 mi (4.2 km), 5060 ft (1542 m), about 1½ hours from the trailhead. Right (south) enters sandy **Lost Canyon** and loops 6.1 mi (9.8 km) back to the trailhead via Squaw Canyon. Continue straight (east-southeast) across the wash, to follow the Peekaboo trail.

After ascending over boulders onto yellow slickrock at 5250 ft (1600 m), the trail heads south and is once again a slickrock route, which it remains until just before the turnaround point at Peekaboo Camp. Wooden Shoe Arch is visible northeast.

Cross a minor **saddle**. Contour right (south-southeast) on red slickrock. Following cairns, curve around the head of a

Pictographs at junction of Peekaboo trail and Salt Creek Canyon

drainage. Then turn left (north) to another **saddle** between knobs—about 15 minutes from the previous, minor saddle. North and South Six-shooter peaks are visible east-northeast.

Cairns lead right (east), descending slightly. Curve into an increasingly astonishing rockscape. The route goes right (south) through a 15-ft (4.6-m) wide **gap**. Descend a chute. Ahead is a towering wall.

Again curving around the head of a slickrock drainage, the route briefly traverses a **very steep slope**. This sharply angled section is short—just a few yards (meters)—but falling here would cause severe injury. Neophytes and acrophobes will be unnerved. If you're hesitant, turn back. Experienced canyon hikers who enjoy friction-walking on precipitous slickrock will proceed—aware but unworried.

Follow cairns curving right to the head of another drainage. Contour north-northeast until reaching the Peekaboo trail's namesake window, at 5360 ft (1634 m). Actually a hole in a fin, the window is just big enough for an adult to scrunch through.

On the other side, curve right (south), then left (east), contouring around the head of yet another drainage. Tall cottonwoods are now visible below (east) in Salt Creek Canyon. Soon, Peekaboo Camp (a backcountry site frequented by four-wheelers) will be visible southeast.

Having hiked about 2½ hours from the trailhead, you're now on a slickrock **arm** that juts into the canyon but is still high above it. Ahead, the route will descend to the canyon floor. Don't turn around to avoid re-ascending. It's worth continuing to see the ancient rock-art panel near Peekaboo Camp.

Hike northeast along the center of the arm, aiming for its end. Angle right, dropping toward the canyon. Near the bottom of the arm, follow a cairn right (south-southeast). Cairns then lead northeast. Still on slickrock, pass low trees to walk under a shallow 10-ft (3-m) high **overhang**. Follow cairns down into a **joint**, where a 15-ft (4.6-m) **ladder** facilitates the final, sheer, 20-ft (6-m) descent.

Immediately beneath the ladder, curve right (southwest) to reach dirt in **Salt Creek Canyon**, at 5070 ft (1545 m). Don't drop the remaining 50 ft (16 m) to the wash bottom. Instead, contour right. Follow a path near the edge of the crumbling, **undercut bank**.

Just before Peekaboo Camp, and slightly above it, there's a large window in the canyon wall (right / west). Right of the window is an impressive **rock-art panel** bearing Fremont shield-figure petroglyphs and handprint pictographs.

Peekaboo Camp, at 5 mi (8.1 km), is just two minutes farther, but it holds no attraction for dayhikers. After appreciating the rock art, return the way you came, enjoying the Peekaboo slickwalk again.

trip 9

upheaval canyon / syncline valley

location	Canyonlands National Park, Island in the Sky District
loop	8 mi (12.9 km)
elevation change	1480-ft (451-m) loss and gain
hiking time	4½ to 6 hours
difficulty	moderate
map	Trails Illustrated *Canyonlands National Park / Needles & Island in the Sky*

opinion

"I have a surprise for you," the earth says. And it always fulfills that promise, everywhere, but not with the frequency and hallucinatory variation that it does in canyon country.

For much of the way along most of the trails in this book, the earth's shapes, colors and textures change with every few steps you take. It's startling yet entrancing. Desert rats unanimously cite this when attempting to explain the mystical allure of canyon-country hiking. And you'll experience it in Upheaval Canyon and Syncline Valley.

Not only is the terrain varied here, but you'll be hiking a loop— forward ever, backward never. And in addition to all the other little surprises along the way, you'll encounter two big ones: abrupt changes in elevation. Early on, the trail plummets off the Island in the Sky, into Upheaval Canyon. Later it surges out of lower Syncline Valley, conniving and muscling its way up a gorge that appears impassable. This intensifies the challenge but makes the journey more interesting.

Desert varnish on walls of Syncline Valley

Be prepared for a hike as demanding as it is dramatic. Expect the initial descent and subsequent ascent to be steep and rugged, though both are brief. The ascent is on a particularly rough route, mildly exposed in two places where a burst of gymnastic effort is necessary to avoid an injurious fall. Alleviate these difficulties—plus gain the benefit of some timely, post-exertion shade—by looping clockwise, as described below. The counter-clockwise hikers we've met here were distressed, admitting the trip was more time-consuming and arduous then they'd anticipated. Which also suggests this shouldn't be your first-ever canyon-country outing; work up to it.

What you'll be looping around is called Upheaval Dome. It's actually a crater. The dome collapsed eons ago—perhaps when struck by a meteor, according to one theory. About midway along the loop, a spur probes the jumbled, eroded moonscape within the crater. It's mildly engaging, but the loop is long enough without adding this 2-mi (3.2-km) round trip. Skip it, unless you're a geologist eager to theorize.

Loopsters also have the option of hiking lower Upheaval Canyon to the White Rim Road—a 7-mi (11.3-km) round trip. The canyon quickly broadens and loses its intrigue. Just up the road from the canyon mouth is Upheaval Campground, but it's reserved for four-wheelers. And the Green River is just a few minutes down-canyon from the road, but it's a placid, unimpressive sight. So skip this excursion too.

Do, however, hike the Upheaval Dome / Crater View spur— an easy, rewarding, 2.5-mi (4-km) round trip. There's little elevation gain or loss. It's mostly on slickrock, so it's fun. The views—of the huge crater below, and the canyons and mesas beyond—are marvelous. And the bird's eye perspective of the crater will satisfy your curiosity, allaying any compulsion to hike into it from the bottom. Ideally, dash out here before starting the Upheaval / Syncline loop. Even the first viewpoint, a mere 0.5-mi (0.8-km) round trip, will enhance your subsequent appreciation of the area.

Though a gratifying hike, Upheaval / Syncline lacks the chief attraction of the Island in the Sky: panoramic vistas. So if you can devote but one day to this district of Canyonlands Park, choose a different trip.

The quick, 0.5-mi (0.8-km) Mesa Arch loop (too short to qualify as a "hike," therefore not in this book) affords a stellar view. (See photo on page 133.) The loop begins near the 27.7-mi (44.6-km) junction described in the *by vehicle* section below. Do it. Then you'll know. If that kind of sweeping, Grand-Canyon-like scenery is your desire, hike the Murphy Hogback (Trip 7) rather than Upheaval / Syncline.

fact

by vehicle

From the junction of Hwys 191 and 128, at the northwest edge of Moab, drive Hwy 191 northwest 8.5 mi (13.7 km) and turn left. From I-70, drive Hwy 191 southeast 20.3 mi (32.7 km) and turn right. From either approach, reset your trip odometer and drive southwest on Hwy 313 signed *Canyonlands, Island in the Sky*.

At 14.5 mi (23.4 km), pass the road to Dead Horse Point State Park (left / east). Shortly beyond, Navajo Mtn and the Henry Mountains are visible on the horizon (right / west).

At 19.2 mi (30.9 km) enter Canyonlands National Park. At 21.6 mi (34.8 km) arrive at the Visitor Center. At the 27.7-mi (44.6-km) junction, go right, toward Upheaval Dome. Reach road's end (picnic tables, toilets, paved trailhead parking area) at 32.5 mi (52.3 km), 5740 ft (1750 m).

on foot

Begin on the signed trail at the west end of the parking area. In one minute, arrive at a four-way **junction**. Straight (northwest) is the Upheaval Dome / Crater View trail, described below. The Syncline trail goes left (west) and right (northeast). Turn left to hike the loop clockwise; it's easier that way. Upon completing the loop, you'll return to this junction.

Heading west, the trail ascends gently for about five minutes, then descends gradually. Within 30 minutes, the trail grants an **overview** of the descent route into Upheaval Canyon. On the left is a bulbous sandstone wall with a cleft down the middle.

An earnest descent begins. Tight switchbacks plunge into a boulder-strewn gully. About 45 minutes from the trailhead, pass a **pouroff** at 4965 ft (1514 m). Bear right (northwest) following cairns up through a small gap. On the other side, resume the steep descent. Your immediate goal, the canyon floor, still looks surprisingly distant. The trail zigzags off ledges, then careens down another bouldery slope.

About an hour from the trailhead, reach the **wash bottom in Upheaval Canyon**, at 4590 ft (1400 m). The wash is usually dry. The trail heads downstream (north-northwest) on sand and gravel, among cottonwoods and junipers. It crosses the wash frequently. Because the wash has cut into the Chinle formation, its banks vary in color: initially rose and steel-blue, later yellow and gray. High above the talus slopes are red-orange Wingate cliffs.

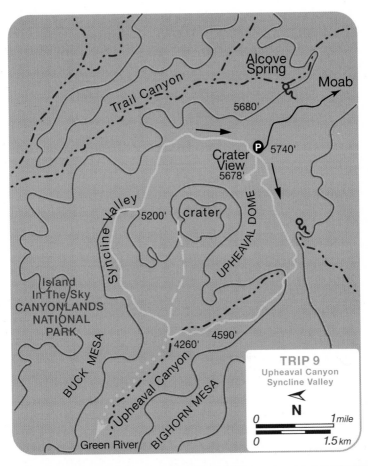

Alcove
Spring

Moab

Trail Canyon

5680'

P 5740'

Crater
View
5678'

Syncline Valley

5200'   crater

UPHEAVAL DOME

Island
In The Sky
CANYONLANDS
NATIONAL
PARK

BUCK MESA

4260'   4590'

Upheaval Canyon

BIGHORN MESA

Green River

TRIP 9
Upheaval Canyon
Syncline Valley

N

0   1 mile
0   1.5 km

Reach a signed **junction** at 3.2 mi (5.2 km), 4260 ft (1300 m), about 1½ hours from the trailhead. This is the confluence of Upheaval Canyon and Syncline Valley. Left (west) follows broad, sandy, brushy Upheaval Canyon generally northwest. It intersects the White Rim Road in 3.5 mi (5.6 km), at 3980 ft (1213 m). It ends 0.25 mi (0.4 km) farther at the Green River. Turn right (north-northeast) into **Syncline Valley** and continue looping around Upheaval Dome. The trail remains on the wash bottom.

Just two minutes from the Upheaval / Syncline confluence junction, the **wash forks** left (northeast) and right (southeast). In both directions, formidable pouroffs are immediately ahead. Proceed between them (directly east), onto a sandy bank. Ascend a steep, manmade **staircase** of pale yellow stone. Attain the bench above.

About eight minutes from the Upheaval / Syncline confluence junction, the trail forks at another signed **junction**. Right (southeast) leads 1.5 mi (2.4 km) into Upheaval Dome crater. Go left (north-northeast) and continue looping around Upheaval Dome.

The trail soon begins ascending boulder-strewn slopes, probing a deep, narrow **gorge** within Syncline Valley. The looming walls and more intimate environment are an intriguing, welcome change.

At 4 mi (6.4 km), about 30 minutes from the Upheaval / Syncline confluence junction, the trail begins climbing steeply over sandstone ledges. Gain 360 ft (110 m) in the next 0.3 mile (0.2 km). This is the exhilarating section of the loop; savor it. At 4700 ft (1433 m) cross to the north-northwest side of the gorge. An **aggressive ascent** ensues among huge boulders. To follow the easiest route, stay attentive.

About five minutes after crossing the gorge, reach a **cable** bolted to a rock wall. It provides a secure handhold, enabling you to swing your leg over a precipice. Two minutes farther, spider-walk up an 8-ft (2.4-m) expanse of **smooth, tilted stone**. The exposure here will unnerve some hikers. Be calm and stable to avoid falling.

Syncline Valley

Having overcome the gorge's two minor difficulties, follow cairns to skirt a large **pouroff**. Regain the wash bottom at 4880 ft (1488 m)—above the pouroff and the gorge below. The going is easy again. The trail heads east, through the **wash**, beneath 500-ft (152-m) walls. During spring or fall afternoons, the walls shade the trail—a relief after an athletic ascent in the sun-exposed gorge. Continue following occasional cairns leading generally northeast.

About an hour from the Upheaval / Syncline confluence junction, the terrain flattens. The trail, now on packed sand, rolls gently through blackbrush. This area is lush in spring, sustaining long grass, wildflowers and creosote bushes. Soon the **canyon forks**. Left (southeast) is impassable. Go right (south) into a narrow, walled channel.

Rise through a rocky section onto a **slickrock cascade**. The trail resumes on loose rock and dirt among boulders left of the

slickrock, but it's more fun to keep ascending the long cascade. Where the slickrock finally pinches out, go up, left, onto the cairned trail. Follow it generally southeast. The imposing, sheer wall left (northeast) of the trail is a spectacle in low-angle, late-afternoon sunlight.

The trail ascends very gently now, through **broad, shallow washes**, amid piñon and juniper forest. It gradually curves south, then southwest. The final stretch of trail parallels the road, which is visible left (south). Keep following cairns over short ledges to arrive at the four-way **junction** where you started the Syncline loop. Right (northwest) is the Upheaval Dome / Crater View trail, described below. Turn left to reach the trailhead parking area in one minute.

upheaval dome / crater view

round trip	2.5 mi (4 km)
elevation gain	300 ft (91 m)
hiking time	15 minutes to 1 hour
difficulty	easy

Begin on the signed trail at the west end of the parking area. In one minute, intersect the Syncline Loop, described above. At this four-way **junction**, go straight (northwest).

About 6 minutes farther, reach a **junction** at 5858 ft (1786 m). Right (north) ends shortly above, at 0.25 mi (0.4 km). This is the **first viewpoint**, atop a small slickrock dome, near the crater's south rim.

Mesa Arch

Proceed left (northwest) from the first viewpoint junction. Follow cairns across slickrock another 8 minutes. At 0.75 mi (1.2 km) reach a **junction**. Ascend right (north), soon topping out at the **second viewpoint**. It's the most impressive, so turn back now if you're short on time or interest.

Continue left (west) from the second viewpoint junction. Descend, curving northwest, beneath the edge of an escarpment. Below, stone steps lead to a **rock-lined trail** across slickrock and gravel. Soon turn right (northeast), rise 5 ft (1.5 m), then drop to the **third viewpoint**. It's behind a pink metal fence, at 5678 ft (1731 m). Having hiked about 20 minutes from the trailhead, you're now on the southwest rim. The crater is 1200 ft (366 m) deep, 1 mi (1.6 km) wide.

From where you last turned to reach the third viewpoint, a **bootbeaten route** continues generally northwest. Follow it 10 minutes farther—on red dirt, among piñon and juniper, left of a pale-rose slickrock convolution. Clamber on broken rock to gaze northwest toward the confluence of Syncline Valley and Upheaval Canyon. You're now 1.25 mi (2 km) from the trailhead. Return the way you came.

trip 10 a, b, c, & d

the needles
chesler park
the joint
devils kitchen
druid arch

location	Canyonlands National Park, Needles District
distances	5.6 mi (9 km) to 15.3 mi (24.6 km)
elevation gain	770 ft (235 m) to 1430 ft (436 m)
hiking time	3 hours to all day
difficulty	easy to moderate
map	Trails Illustrated *Canyonlands National Park / Needles & Island in the Sky*

opinion

Until you can vacation on distant planets, there's always Canyonlands National Park—a land as other-worldly as it gets without requiring a space suit to step out of your vehicle. This group of hikes penetrates the Needles—a concentration of fantastic redrock formations (pinnacles, fins, domes, hamburger buns, mushrooms, flying saucers) dominating the park's southern half.

Though the Needles are solid rock, their incomprehensible complexity gives the appearance of movement, vibration, dance. Perhaps because they keep your eyes darting from one implausible shape to the next. Perhaps because each intricate detail flows seamlessly, endlessly into another. Perhaps because you're indeed witnessing earth's living drama—a slower

The Needles, Canyonlands National Park

episode than a waterfall, a storm, or a volcanic eruption, but equally dynamic. Gazing at the Needles is like watching a jazz dance troupe writhing on stage: it's impossible to see every nuance, yet you try, because it's all so fascinating.

These four hikes begin at Elephant Hill trailhead. It's a busy place. A 4WD road departs here, and—despite all the hiking options—there's initially just one trail. But the 4WD road immediately veers in the opposite direction, and the trail soon branches into a web allowing hikers to disperse. It's possible to see it all—light and fast—in two or three dayhikes. The various round trips and circuits accommodate any schedule or energy level.

trip 10a – the needles, chesler park overlook

As its name suggests, Chesler Park is a broad, level expanse of desert grasses. The surrounding Needles make it special. The park's north side abuts the Needles' most intense concentration. Very near that north side is a pass affording a superb view. And the canyonscape en route to the pass is captivating. Round trip: 5.6 mi (9 km).

trip 10b – the needles, chesler park, the joint

Continue through the pass overlooking Chesler Park, then loop around the park's outer edge. You'll visit the Joint, where a slim corridor through fractured rock offers a hiking experience worthy of Mordor. And you'll return immediately beneath the Needles' most bizarre cluster. Circuit: 11.1 mi (17.9 km).

trip 10c – the needles, chesler park, the joint, devils kitchen

After rounding the north edge Chesler Park, beneath the Needles' most outrageous upsurge, return via Devils Kitchen. The Kitchen has a 4WD-accessible campground, so it's not a destination for hikers but merely a waypoint on the journey. The entire trek is through enthralling Needles scenery. Circuit: 10.5 mi (16.9 km).

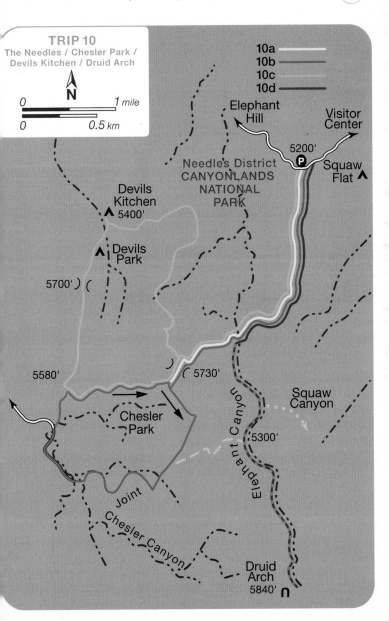

TRIP 10
The Needles / Chesler Park /
Devils Kitchen / Druid Arch

↑ N

0 _____ 1 mile

0 _____ 0.5 km

10a ━━━
10b ━━━
10c ━━━
10d ━━━

Elephant
Hill

Visitor
Center

5200'
Ⓟ

Squaw
Flat ⛺

Needle's District
CANYONLANDS
NATIONAL
PARK

Devils
Kitchen
⛰ 5400'

⛰ Devils
Park

5700') (

5580'

Chesler
Park

) (5730'

Squaw
Canyon

5300'

Elephant Canyon

Joint

Chesler Canyon

Druid
Arch
5840' ∩

Spring storm over the Needles

trip 10d – druid arch

Druids were members of an ancient Celtic priesthood. In Irish and Welsh sagas and Christian legends, druids appear as magicians or wizards. The name *Druid Arch* is wildly inventive, yet bang on. The arch, strongly evocative of Stonehenge, feels like the work of a primeval, esoteric cult. The trail to this natural monument probes the slabby wash of Elephant Canyon. It culminates with a short, vigorous scamper onto the canyon's sandstone benches. Round trip: 10.8 mi (17.4 km). Strong hikers can vary the return and see more new terrain by cutting over to Chesler Park, visiting the Joint, and completing a 15.3-mi (24.6-km) circuit gaining 1430 ft (436 m).

fact

before your trip

If you intend to dayhike in the area for a few days, try to camp at Squaw Flat. The campground has water (spring through

Chesler Park and more needles

fall) and toilets. The 26 sites, each with picnic table and fire pit, are available first come, first served. If the campground's full—which it usually is during peak season—arrive by 10 a.m., watch for someone to leave, then claim their vacated site.

by vehicle

From Moab, drive Hwy 191 south 38.5 mi (62 km). Or, from Monticello, drive Hwy 191 north 13.5 mi (21.7 km). From either approach, turn west onto Hwy 211, signed *Canyonlands National Park, Needles District.* (A few miles north of this junction is a road west signed *Needles Overlook*, which is *not* your destination.)

Heading west on Hwy 211, pass Newspaper Rock—a must see—at 12.3 mi (19.8 km). Reach the Visitor Center at 35 mi (56.4 km). Continue another 2.5 mi (4 km) generally southwest following signs for Squaw Flat Campground.

Bear right where left enters campground loop A. Shortly beyond, stay straight where left enters campground loop B. Proceed another 3 mi (5 km) on an unpaved but well-maintained 2WD road to the Elephant Hill trailhead parking area, at 5200 ft (1585 m).

on foot

trip 10a – the needles, chesler park overlook

Round trip	5.6 mi (9 km)
Elevation gain	770 ft (235 m)

The trail departs the southwest side of the parking area, left of where a technical 4WD road begins climbing. Follow the trail generally south. Ascend stone **stairs** through a **cleft** to reach 5360 ft (1634 m). Proceed on the now sandy, gravelly trail among peculiar sandstone formations. Pass left of redrock walls. About 30 minutes from the trailhead, a 40-ft (12-m) high slickrock **bench** at 5420 ft (1652 m) offers a superb view of the Needles just 300 yd (330 m) ahead.

After a gentle descent, reach a **junction** at 1.5 mi (2.4 km) among piñon, juniper and rabbitbrush. Left (east-southeast) leads 3.5 mi (5.6 km) to Squaw Flat Campground. Go right (southwest) to reach Chesler Park in 1.4 mi (2.3 km) and Druid Arch in 3.9 mi (6.3 km).

The trail hops onto slickrock, progressing between fins on slickrock buttes. Slip through a joint in the rock. Drop into an inner, redrock canyon alive with twisted juniper. Reach a **junction** at 2.1 mi (3.4 km), 5300 ft (1616 m), in **Elephant Canyon**. Left (south), up the canyon wash, leads 3.3 mi (5.3 km) to Druid Arch. For this trip, however, cross the wash and follow the trail right (west).

A moderate ascent weaves among boulders and juniper. Reach another **junction** at 2.7 mi (4.3 km), 5570 ft (1698 m), amid impressive pinnacles and fins rising 500 ft (152 m). Straight (north-northwest) leads 2.3 mi (3.8 km) to Devils Kitchen; you'll return that way on Trip 10c. For this trip, go left (southwest).

A steep ascent on loose rock and slickrock in a gully between fins, climaxes at a small, 5730-ft (1747-m) **pass**. Having hiked 2.8 mi (4.5 km) from the trailhead, you're now smack against the Needles' east end, overlooking Chesler Park—a plain of sand, grass, and rabbitbrush. Southwest are sandstone mushrooms and buns, and a scattering of standing stones. The sandy trail drops to a junction below, on the edge of Chesler Park, but for this shorter trip descend just part way. Drop your pack, relax on the slickrock, nosh your rye crisp and Emmenthal cheese, and devour the view. Return the way you came. Your total round-trip distance will be 5.6 mi (9 km).

trip 10b – the needles, chesler park, the joint

Circuit	11.1 mi (17.9 km)
Elevation gain	910 ft (277 m)

Follow the directions for Trip 10a above. From the **pass** at 2.8 mi (4.5 km), proceed down the sandy trail to the **junction** at 2.9 mi (4.7 km), on the edge of Chesler Park. Right (west-southwest) grazes the south edge of the Needles, en route to Devils Kitchen (Trip 10c). For this trip, however, turn left (southeast) and begin looping around Chesler Park.

Reach a **junction** at 4.2 mi (6.8 km). Left leads 1 mi (1.6 km) generally east to intersect the Elephant Canyon trail north of Druid Arch. Bear right (south-southwest).

Soon pass backcountry **campsite** CP2 (sheltered between giant boulders) and a spur right (northwest) accessing three more campsites. At 4.9 mi (7.9 km) approach **the Joint**. It's a fissure: deep, narrow, long, shady, cool. The path inside is sandy and brush-free. Slipping through this rock-walled slot is fun for all but claustrophobes. Upon exiting, cairns lead right (northwest). Descend through more rock curiosities to a **4WD road** at 5.7 mi (9.2 km).

Follow the road northwest 0.5 mi (0.8 km)—about 15 minutes. At 6.2 mi (10 km) bear right (north-northeast) onto a trail signed *Devils Kitchen*. The sign is just off the road, near where the road curves left / west.

The Joint

Ascend through sandstone lumps to a **junction** at 7 mi (11.3 km). Left (northwest) leads to Devils Kitchen (Trip 10c). Go right (east), beneath the most concentrated section of the Needles.

At 8.2 mi (13.2 km) arrive at the **junction** immediately south of and below the pass, where you began looping around Chesler Park. You're now on familiar ground. Return the way you came. Your total circuit distance will be 11.1 mi (17.9 km).

trip 10c – the needles, chesler park, devils kitchen

Circuit	10.5 mi (16.9 km)
Elevation gain	1060 ft (323 m)

Follow the directions for Trip 10 a and b. From the **pass** at 2.8 mi (4.5 km), proceed down the sandy trail to the **junction** at 2.9 mi (4.7 km), on the edge of Chesler Park. Left (southeast) leads to the Joint (Trip 10b). For this trip, however, go right (west-southwest), beneath the south edge of the the Needles.

Reach a sandy **junction** at 4.1 mi (6.6 km), 5580 ft (1700 m). Left (south-southwest) is the return route from the Joint. Go right (northwest). Ascend a defile between walls. Continue on rock and sand to a small, 5700-ft (1738-m) **pass**.

Descend north—on rock stairs, then beneath an overhanging ledge. Enter Devils Park, a level, sandy area (similar to Chesler Park, but smaller) ringed by mushroom formations. About 30 minutes from the last junction, pass a right spur accessing

Druid Arch

backcountry **campsite** DP1, at 5500 ft (1677 m) behind a fin. Proceed generally north-northeast on the sandy, main trail, descending slightly, parallel to and left of a 100-ft (30-m) wall. At 5.5 mi (8.9 km), about 15 minutes from the campsite spur, arrive at **Devils Kitchen** backcountry campground, also accessible by 4WD. It has toilets, and a large, flat boulder shaded by a juniper—perfect for a lounging rest stop.

To resume, go around the juniper, keeping the toilet on your left. Ahead is a table beneath an overhanging boulder. The hiking trail leads east. Be sure you're not heading north on the 4WD road. Left of the trail are intriguing caverns in bulbous sandstone walls.

After ascending a slickrock pouroff, the trail rolls along on slickrock and sand, past juniper and piñon, through fins and pinnacles, to the head of another drainage. At 7.8 mi (12.6 km), about an hour from Devils Kitchen, reach a **junction** at 5570 ft (1698 m), amid impressive pinnacles and fins rising 500 ft

(152 m). This is immediately northeast of and below the pass you crossed to enter Chesler Park. You're now on familiar ground. Go left (east-southeast) to return the way you came. Your total circuit distance will be 10.5 mi (16.9 km).

trip 10d – druid arch

Round trip	10.8 mi (17.4 km)
Elevation gain	880 ft (268 m)

Follow the directions for Trip 10a until the **junction** at 2.1 mi (3.4 km), 5300 ft (1616 m), in **Elephant Canyon**. Across the wash, right (west) leads to the Needles, Chesler Park, The Joint, and Devils Kitchen. For this trip, however, go left (south), up the canyon wash.

Reach a **junction** at 2.9-mi (4.7-km). Left (southeast) leads to Big Spring Canyon (Trip 5). Go right (south-southeast) for Druid Arch.

At 3.4 mi (5.5 km) reach another **junction**. Go left (southeast) for Druid Arch. Right leads 1 mi (1.6 km) generally west to a junction on the southeast edge of Chesler Park, near the Joint. If you go that way after seeing the arch, and then follow directions for Trip 10b, you'll complete a 15.3-mi (24.6-km) tour.

In a few minutes, at a convergence of washes, go left into the larger wash, toward higher canyon walls. The remaining 0.75 mi (1.2 km) is on a bench above the wash. Reach the base of **Druid Arch** at 5.4 mi (8.7 km), 5840 ft (1780 m). When the fin end of the stalwart 500-ft (152-m) high arch is visible, follow cairns ascending left onto a white rim. Climb a metal ladder. The fin is above you, immediately ahead. To attain the optimal viewpoint, the route ascends another 80 ft (24 m) above the rim. The going is rough but should pose no danger to sure-footed hikers.

Admire the arch while savoring your tuna-on-a-bagel sandwich, then return the way you came. Your total round-trip distance will be 10.8 mi (17.4 km).

INFORMATION SOURCES

Arches National Park
(435) 719-2299
www.nps.gov/arch

Canyonlands National Park
(435) 719-2313
www.nps.gov/cany

Moab Information Center
corner of Main and Center streets
(435) 259-8825 or (800) 635-6622
www.discovermoab.com

Weather
www.moabadventurecenter.com/weather

INDEX

Colorado River, from Highway 128

Canyonlands National Park, from the Slickrock trail

THE AUTHORS

Kathy and Craig are dedicated to each other, and to hiking, in that order. Their second date was a 32-km (20-mile) dayhike in Arizona. Since then they haven't stopped for long.

They've trekked through much of the world's vertical topography, including the Himalayas, Patagonian Andes, Spanish Pyrenees, Swiss Alps, Scottish Highlands, Italian Dolomites, and New Zealand Alps. In North America, they've explored the B.C. Coast, Selkirk and Purcell ranges, Montana's Beartooth Wilderness, Wyoming's Grand Tetons, the California Sierra, Washington's North Cascades, and the Colorado Rockies.

In 1989 they moved from the U.S. to Canada, so they could live near the Canadian Rockies—the range that inspired the first of their refreshingly unconventional guidebooks: *Don't Waste Your Time in the Canadian Rockies, The Opinionated Hiking Guide.*

Its popularity encouraged them to abandon their careers—Kathy as an ESL teacher, Craig as an ad-agency creative director—and start their own guidebook publishing company: hikingcamping.com.

Though the distances they hike are epic, Kathy and Craig agree that hiking, no matter how far, is the easiest of the many tasks necessary to create a guidebook. What they find most challenging is having to sit at their Canmore, Alberta, home, with the Canadian Rockies visible out the window. But they do it every winter, spending twice as much time at their computers—writing, organizing, editing, checking facts—as they do on the trail.

The result is worth it. Kathy and Craig's colourful writing, opinionated commentary, and enthusiasm for the joys of hiking make their guidebooks uniquely helpful and compelling.

Other Titles from hikingcamping.com

The following titles—boot-tested and written by the Opinionated Hikers, Kathy & Craig Copeland—are widely available in outdoor shops and bookstores. Visit www.hikingcamping.com to read excerpts and purchase online. The website also offers updates for each book, recent reports on trails and campsites, and details about new titles such as the *Done in a Day* series.

Don't Waste Your Time in the Canadian Rockies®
The Opinionated Hiking Guide

ISBN 0-9689419-7-4 Even here, in a mountain range designated a UNESCO World Heritage Site for its "superlative natural phenomena" and "exceptional natural beauty and aesthetic importance," not all scenery is equal. Some destinations are simply more striking, more intriguing, more inspiring than others. Now you can be certain you're choosing a rewarding hike for your weekend or vacation. This uniquely helpful, visually captivating guidebook covers Banff, Jasper, Kootenay, Yoho and Waterton Lakes national parks, plus Mt. Robson and Mt. Assiniboine provincial parks. It rates each trail *Premier, Outstanding, Worthwhile,* or *Don't Do*, explains why, and provides comprehensive route descriptions. 138 dayhikes and backpack trips. Trail maps for each hike. 544 pages, 270 photos, full colour throughout. 5th edition updated July 2006.

Where Locals Hike
in the Canadian Rockies
The Premier Trails in Kananaskis
Country, near Canmore and Calgary

ISBN 978-0-9783427-4-6 The 55 most
rewarding dayhikes and backpack
trips within two hours of Calgary's
international airport. All lead to
astonishing alpine meadows, ridges
and peaks. Though these trails are
little known compared to those in the
nearby Canadian Rocky Mountain
national parks, the scenery is equally
magnificent. Includes Peter Lougheed
and Spray Valley provincial parks. Discerning trail reviews
help you choose your trip. Detailed route descriptions keep
you on the path. 320 pages, 180 photos, trail maps for each
hike, full colour throughout. Updated 3rd edition August 2008.

Where Locals Hike
in the West Kootenay
The Premier Trails in Southeast B.C.
near Kaslo & Nelson

ISBN 978-0-9689419-9-7 See the
peaks, glaciers and cascades that
make locals passionate about these
mountains. The 50 most rewarding
dayhikes and backpack trips in the
Selkirk and west Purcell ranges of
southeast British Columbia. Includes
Valhalla, Kokanee Glacier, and Goat
Range parks, as well as hikes near
Arrow, Slocan, and Kootenay lakes. Discerning trail reviews
help you choose your trip. Detailed route descriptions keep
you on the path. 272 pages, 130 photos, trail locator maps, full
colour throughout. Updated 2nd edition April 2007.

Camp Free in B.C.

ISBN 978-0-9735099-3-9 Make your weekend or vacation adventurous and revitalizing. Enjoy British Columbia's scenic byways and 2WD backroads—in your low-clearance car or your big RV. Follow precise directions to 350 campgrounds, from the B.C. Coast to the Rocky Mountains. Choose from 80 low-fee campgrounds similar in quality to provincial parks but half the price. Find retreats where the world is

yours alone. Simplify life: slow down, ease up. Fully appreciate B.C.'s magnificent backcountry, including the Sunshine Coast, Okanagan, Shuswap Highlands, Selkirk and Purcell ranges, Cariboo Mountains, and Chilcotin Plateau. 544 pages, 200 photos, 20 regional maps, full colour throughout. Updated 4th edition April 2007.

Gotta Camp Alberta

ISBN 978-0-9735099-0-8 Make your weekend or vacation adventurous and revitalizing. Enjoy Alberta's scenic byways and 2WD backroads—in your low-clearance car or your big RV. Follow precise directions to 150 idyllic campgrounds, from the foothill lakes to the Rocky Mountains. Camp in national parks, provincial parks, and recreation areas. Find retreats where the world is yours alone. Simplify life: slow down, ease up.

Return home soothed by the serenity of nature. Approximately 400 pages, 170 photos, and 18 maps. Full colour throughout. First edition June 2008.

Hiking from Here to WOW:
North Cascades
50 Trails to the Wonder of Wilderness

ISBN 978-0-89997-444-6 The authors
hiked more than 1,400 miles through
North Cascades National Park plus
the surrounding wilderness areas,
including Glacier Peak, Mt. Baker,
and the Pasayten. They took more
than 1,000 photos and hundreds of
pages of field notes. Then they culled
their list of favourite hikes down to
50 trips—each selected for its power
to incite awe. Their 264-page book describes where to find
the cathedral forests, psychedelic meadows, spiky summits,
and colossal glaciers that distinguish the American Alps. And
it does so in refreshing style: honest, literate, entertaining,
inspiring. Like all *WOW Guides*, this one is full colour
throughout, with 180 photos and a trail map for each dayhike
and backpack trip. First edition May 2007.

Hiking from Here to WOW:
Utah Canyon Country
90 Trails to the Wonder of Wilderness

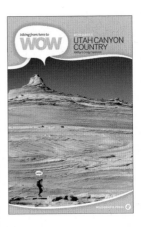

ISBN 978-0-89997-452-1 The authors
hiked more than 1,600 miles through
Zion, Bryce, Escalante-Grand Staircase,
Glen Canyon, Grand Gulch, Cedar
Mesa, Canyonlands, Moab, Arches,
Capitol Reef, and the San Rafael Swell.
They took more than 2,500 photos and
hundreds of pages of field notes. Then
they culled their list of favourite hikes
down to 90 trips—each selected for its
power to incite awe. Their 480-page book describes where to
find the redrock cliffs, slickrock domes, soaring arches, and

ancient ruins that make southern Utah unique in all the world. And it does so in refreshing style: honest, literate, entertaining, inspiring. Like all *WOW Guides*, this one is full colour throughout, with 220 photos and a trail map for each dayhike and backpack trip. First edition April 2008.

Done in a Day: Jasper
The 10 Premier Hikes

ISBN 978-0-9783427-1-5 Where to invest your limited hiking time to enjoy the greatest scenic reward. Choose an easy, vigourous, or challenging hike. Start your adventure within a short drive of town. Witness the wonder of Jasper National Park and be back for a hot shower, great meal, and soft bed. 128 pages, 75 photos, trail maps for each trip, full colour throughout. First edition December 2007.

Done in a Day: Banff
The 10 Premier Hikes

ISBN 978-0-9783427-0-8 Where to invest your limited hiking time to enjoy the greatest scenic reward. Choose an easy, vigourous, or challenging hike. Start your adventure within a short drive of town. Witness the wonder of Banff National Park and be back for a hot shower, great meal, and soft bed. 136 pages, 90 photos, trail maps for each trip, full colour throughout. First edition December 2007.

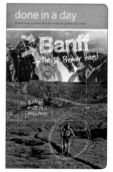

Done in a Day: Whistler
The 10 Premier Hikes

ISBN 978-0-9735099-7-7 Where to invest your limited hiking time to enjoy the greatest scenic reward. Choose an easy, vigourous, or challenging hike. Start your adventure within a short drive of the village. Witness the wonder of Whistler, British Columbia, and be back for a hot shower, great meal, and soft bed. 144 pages, 80 photos, trail maps for each trip, full colour throughout. First edition December 2007.

Done in a Day: Calgary
The 10 Premier Road Rides

ISBN 978-0-9783427-3-9 Where to invest your limited cycling time to enjoy the greatest scenic reward. Spring through fall, southwest Alberta offers cyclists blue-ribbon road riding: from alpine passes in the Canadian Rockies, to dinosaur-country river canyons on the edge of the prairie. And this compact, jersey-pocket-sized book is your guide to the crème de la crème: the ten most serene, compelling, bike-friendly roads in the region. Start pedaling within a short drive of Calgary. At day's end, be back for a hot shower, great meal, and soft bed. 120 pages, 80 photos, road maps for each ride, full colour throughout. First edition December 2007.

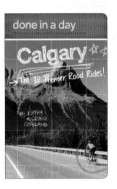